ADVANCE PRAISE FOR

Explorations in Contemporary Feminist Literature

"Incisive reflections that develop new perspectives on vital issues in contemporary feminist literature. Engaging and clearly written."

Jeffner Allen, Professor of Philosophy and Women's Studies, Binghamton University, New York

"In her provocative book, Mary Pernal contributes to a growing body of literature exploring an expanded feminist consciousness that looks at how race and transgendered experience continue to challenge our conceptualizations of 'women.'"

Leslie Heywood, Associate Professor of English and Cultural Studies, Binghamton University, New York

"This is a highly original study of the intersections between gender identity, politics, and spirituality containing outstanding analysis of literary texts. Mary Pernal's writing is detailed, lively, jargon-free, and remarkably in topic. Her work coalesces in the way art does."

Susan Strehle, Professor of English, Binghamton University, New York

"Mary Pernal's book keeps opening doors into new dimensions of her subject. Her insistent reconfiguring of the interface between reader and text is refreshing and bracing. She creates an artful, tightly framed and provocative cultural challenge."

Ann Boehm, Senior Lecturer, Writing Department, Cornell University, New York

Explorations in Contemporary Feminist Literature

ERUPTIONS
New Thinking across the Disciplines

Erica McWilliam
General Editor

Vol. 15

PETER LANG
New York • Washington, D.C./Baltimore • Bern
Frankfurt am Main • Berlin • Brussels • Vienna • Oxford

Mary Pernal

Explorations in Contemporary Feminist Literature

The Battle against Oppression for Writers of Color, Lesbian and Transgender Communities

PETER LANG
New York • Washington, D.C./Baltimore • Bern
Frankfurt am Main • Berlin • Brussels • Vienna • Oxford

Library of Congress Cataloging-in-Publication Data

Pernal, Mary.
Explorations in contemporary feminist literature: the battle against oppression for writers of color, lesbian and transgender communities / Mary Pernal.
p. cm. — (Eruptions; vol. 15)
Includes bibliographical references.
1. American literature—Women authors—History and criticism. 2. Feminism and literature—United States—History—20th century. 3. Women and literature—United States—History—20th century. 4. American literature—Minority authors—History and criticism. 5. American literature—20th century—History and criticism. 6. Lesbians' writings, American—History and criticism. 7. Transsexuals in literature. 8. Minorities in literature. 9. Lesbians in literature. 10. Oppression (Psychology) I. Title. II. Series.
PS228.F45 P47 810.9'9287'0904—dc21 2001029583
ISBN 0-8204-5662-4
ISSN 1091-8590

Die Deutsche Bibliothek-CIP-Einheitsaufnahme

Pernal, Mary:
Explorations in contemporary feminist literature: the battle against oppression for writers of color, lesbian and transgender communities / Mary Pernal.
–New York; Washington, D.C./Baltimore; Bern;
Frankfurt am Main; Berlin; Brussels; Vienna; Oxford: Lang.
(Eruptions; Vol. 15)
ISBN 0-8204-5662-4

Cover design by Joni Holst

Table of Contents

Introduction

This book is a journey through the writings of a selection of contemporary women writers; its intention is to reveal the powerful messages and theoretical arguments underlying their personal narratives and works of fiction. The writers are from diverse multicultural and class backgrounds and have diverse gender identities and preferences. The common in their work could most easily be expressed as a combination of a direct and convincing writing style and an underlying social commentary on the need to unearth and recognize injustice, violence, and oppression to facilitate the transformation of entrenched and destructive societal patterns. I have been drawn to writers who wish to break the silence.

Writing is a necessity for certain people; for them it is not a lofty exercise, hobby, or pastime. Nor is it merely the spinning of beautiful tales with volumes of eloquent exposition. Their writing is the expression of cultural and personal truths that have been covered over and suppressed by an oppressive historical view that has been carried over into the present day. It is a rebellion against colonial domination and its aftermath.

The essays of Audre Lorde have been my guiding light for this project, particularly her "Poetry Is Not a Luxury" from *Sister Outsider*. I have set out to examine the power of fiction and personal writing to convey truthful, accurate, and careful perceptions of diverse life experiences. Rather than bare intellectual data, I am interested here in writing that insists that the reader reflect, remember, and take in the impact of writers' experiences of neglect and abuse so that the reality of oppression and its consequences will be felt and realized more deeply. The power of writing to shake us out of numb acceptance of the status quo, regardless of our position in society in terms of race, class, gender identity, or preference, can serve to propel the reader toward a process of continuous self-reflection and critical thinking about our society's social values and roots. Such reflection can undermine unconscious prejudices and assumptions. It is also the ground from which the connections in the messages of different authors, speakers, activists, and thinkers become evident; it often resonates across vast experiential and varying thought processes. A message of justice links a coalition of individuals and groups, creating hope for future collective transformation.

I hope that my own participation in this process is evident in my approach to reading these authors. My interpretations and particular points of interest are shaped by my own experiences. I make no claim to objectivity in this work and no claim that my interpretations unearth an ultimate and irrefutable meaning in the texts I study. I acknowledge the individuality of each writer, and the fact that they wrote for their own purposes—not mine. In that sense, this treatise is a written dialogue and discussion. I see these authors as teachers as well as craftspersons of a wonderful and delightful art form.

I originally started this book with the idea that transgendered perspectives (specifically f-t-m—female to male) would offer new insights into age-old feminist issues. Perhaps conflating the term "transgender" with transcendence, I assumed that anyone pushing the boundaries that define female gender was necessarily engaged in a feminist transformation of social values. I assumed that an ideological process of expansion, and of tolerance, was a necessary component of a gender transition. I thought that the transformation of outward gender characteristics was innately connected to the inner acceptance of the many possible gendered identities of others. I felt that an exploration of this process could have consequences for a broad spectrum of people and could apply to anyone with gender openness or variation, to feminist projects, and even to race-oriented and class-oriented civil rights projects, since the issues are quite similar in the final analysis; that is, that a struggle is taking place against a normative construction that specifically excludes diverse communities in order to guarantee special status, privilege, and authority for a particular class of individuals who pass themselves off as neutral uncircumscribed subjects and rest in the uneasy and purposeful delusion that their rights are ordinary rather than exclusively privileged. The loose conglomeration of privileged individuals I refer to may see themselves as exclusively white, upper-class, heterosexual, male, Christian, American, or any combination or addition that is invoked for the expressed purpose of excluding from recognition women, lesbian women, women of color, impoverished women, transgendered individuals, or individuals whose values deviate from the dominant paradigm.

As a result of such reflections, the focus of my project broadened considerably to include issues of identity based on race, class, and sexual preferences while still addressing a selection of contemporary fictional literature on f-t-m transgendered identity from a feminist perspective. I had to overcome several assumptions. First, rather than demand that every individual who presents his/her outer gender at variance to heterosexual male/female normative expectations be seen as consciously transgressive, as a person purposely seeking to transform the narrow laws of a restrictive culture, it seems more realistic to acknowledge that people make decisions for their own reasons. They are sometimes informed by a political or ideological agenda...and sometimes not. In Rose Tremain's novel *Sacred Country,* a transgendered character is presented who is, in fact, undergoing a feminist revolution through her physical transformation to a more masculine body. An investigation of the theoretical and psychological motivations behind her identification as a male and eventual surgery, forms much of the dramatic content of the novel. Other authors, however, have a different goal in presenting transgendered characters. *Stone Butch Blues,* by Leslie Feinberg, for instance, presents a believable lifelike character whose male identity is a given rather than a subject of psychological investigation, as does Frankie Hucklenbroich's novel *A Crystal Diary*.

Unlike Tremain, these authors share the goal of asserting the right of individuals to exist in a male gender that is either considered innately present or whose psychological origins are irrelevant to the issue at hand. Their primary concern is the political right of individuals to freedom of gender and sexual expression. As a result, a critique of feminism's role in the formation of the characters' identity, and vice versa, is almost entirely missing from their novels, perhaps out of an unwarranted fear that such an analysis would undermine the seeming solidity of the characters' identities by suggesting that they are shaped by cultural forces and therefore that their gender expression is somehow arbitrary.

The origins of this rigid, but practical, position are obvious: it is a response to the familiar litany of those who falsely argue that homosexuality and transgendered identities are the result of aberrations and illness. The idea that identity is formed rather than innate can seem to threaten the legitimacy of variant genders. The parent who asks "Where did I go wrong?" echoes views long held in psychological fields regarding homosexuality and transgendered identity. And yet the claim that gender is socially formed and defined, at least in part, does not necessarily imply that gender is arbitrary, or even free and unfixed. To the contrary, very fixed notions of gender exist within culture and are culturally produced through sanctioned roles assigned to gender. The result is that even for transgendered individuals the ideas that shape gender can be quite rigid. In the hope that we can escape the shame-generating biases of socially imposed rigid views of gender, I believe that any project aimed at increasing an open-minded acceptance of gender variability, whether in the individual or in society, must entail extensive careful and critical analysis and introspection regarding the social construction of gender. I must acknowledge, however, that the political and theoretical project of generating open-minded tolerance of gender expression does not necessarily create that reality for the individual existing in intolerant surroundings as a gender-variant individual, even though I have the bias that it should do so.

Of the authors mentioned above, only Tremain is specifically interested in unearthing social forces at play in cultural readings of gender. As a result, her character comes across as fictional—the product of theoretical ruminations rather than lived recorded experience. I found myself in a quandary. My interest in the subject of transgender identity is feminist, and admittedly theoretical. As a feminist, I am deeply interested in discovering the mechanisms at work that define gender on a cultural level, and I am keenly invested in revealing biased and limited definitions that prioritize male existence while erasing the significance of female existence. I am likewise interested in investigating the mechanisms of discrimination at play in the denigration of the position of womanhood and, furthermore, in unearthing the enforced demarcations separating women's existence from male existence, since such distinctions are used to reinforce the subjugation of women to a lesser, subservient position. There is no doubt that this theoretical stance puts me at odds with several authors who explore f-t-m transgendered existence from a standpoint that seeks to highlight gender distinctions and to imbue even subtle gender markers with deep, even innate, significance.

The second consideration that shaped this project was a growing need I felt to draw connections between various forms of discrimination, specifically discrimination against women. For my purposes, the original focus on transgender issues exclusively proved to be too narrow to adequately address the many factors I saw at work in privileging a particular position of what might be termed the center, from which all other identities are marginalized and read as inadequate. I chose, therefore, to address a broad array of experiences of discrimination described by a variety of late twentieth-century writers, predominantly women and, more important, to explore the process of answering from a perspective that is able to rearrange the powerful worldview habitually presented within dominant ideology.

"Twentieth-Century Multicultural Women Writers of North America" gives an overview of a selection of techniques used by women writers to critique cultural biases in terms of race, class, gender, and issues of lesbian identity. It also demonstrates how the historical developments of feminism are reflected in the changing characters and social contexts presented by women authors whose work spans the past century.

"Resistance and Liberation" presents issues of racism in detail and is one of the few sections of the book to include male authors. It also addresses the work of Maya Angelou and explores the spiritual grounding that sustains individuals threatened with oppression and, in some cases, annihilation.

"Expanding the Parameters of Feminism: Self-Healing in Toni Morrison's *Paradise*" focuses on a feminist interpretation of *Paradise* that takes into account race and other issues that complicate the picture of feminism. Although unity in diversity is absolutely necessary to oppose overwhelming oppression, coalitions are often broken apart by individual differences and aims. The ways in which an individual must fight to sustain herself are often shown to be at odds with sustaining a community.

"The Transformative Power of Personal Voice: Students' Rights to Free Expression" explores my attemptes to create feminist classroom environments conducive to teaching radical and multicultural writers in a way that effectively educates and empowers students. My goal as an educator is to create a feminist classroom, which also means a classroom in which diversity of all kinds is accepted and appreciated. I pay special attention in this chapter to the complications that can arise in a classroom in which all voices are heard and to the benefits of demonstrating to students the importance and power of their own voices by asking them to call on their past experiences and mature insights. In effect, I ask them to trust their own voices, which in some sense, I suspect, is the project of every feminist and progressive author included in a multicultural curriculum.

"Reflections on Alternative Identities in Contemporary Feminism: S&M and Butch/Femme Cultures" addresses transgender and sexually rebellious characterizations of women and examines the significance of these identities in terms of resistance. In some respects it grows out of the topics of earlier chapters, but it represents later thoughts on the debate over whether an attitude of cultural resistance is always and necessarily a feminist act. Predictably, my answer turns out to be "yes and no," with a marked evolution from my previous inclination to say "no." My motivation in returning to the works of Pat Califia, Leslie Feinberg, Rose Tremain, and others is to do justice to the impact that contemporary gender-feminist writing has had on feminist culture, while maintaining a steady critical look at hidden assumptions (my own included).

Writers on race, such as Audre Lorde, bell hooks, Maya Angelou, and Toni Morrison, have made it clear that the workings of society need to be constantly and carefully examined so that we, as individuals and as a feminist community, can rework and undo the damage now inflicted on many people today through oppression and discrimination. In the case of gender, I wish to caution against silencing feminist voices who express concerns about sexism that may be encountered even in relationships between women in lesbian, butch-femme, or S&M paradigms. While my earlier chapters on gender celebrate the unyielding courage behind specific outspoken public acts of protest and free expression, this chapter examines the varying motivations and sometimes troubling effects of different stances.

Women's gendered exclusion from male rights—specifically the privileged male position of subjective presence and its analog, the defined status of women as specifically absent, missing, estranged, and inadequate in comparison to male status (in order, as a shadow, to highlight its being)—bears many similarities to politically motivated race distinctions laid forth to erase the significance of identities other than white. Power relationships have been imposed on these identities and therefore come to exist as part of these relationships. In the dominant paradigm, "male" and "white" have become inextricable from subjectivity, power, dominance, prominence, authority, and so on, and "female" and "color" have become inextricable from objectivity, accommodation, self-effacement, and non-presence.

The concept of masculinity itself is therefore constructed on some level as white, straight, and economically empowered, so that anyone lacking these qualities finds his/her authority and subjective right of presence questioned. Her/his "right" to throw off any shadow of self-effacement and to see the world as literally hers/his for the taking, as existing for her/him alone, is incomplete (perhaps thankfully). It means that her/his status is less than that of the emperor-like absolute power by held heroic and mythic figures who are characterized as white, male, educated, wealthy, and in a position of inherited or proclaimed authority over other people's lives and livelihoods.

If this were all there was to the picture, we would all simply despair. And yet the authors addressed in this project point out that masculinity is not inherently dominant. The same is true for race. And though despair and weariness are in fact present in many people's lives, people survive, and in this fact there is hope for the future even when the present has its grim side. Perhaps an "outsider" can create a vision of a better life and in some sense bring it into being through expression in thought, action, and speech. It enhances human dignity to read the stories of individuals when they are presented as significant and meaningful.

In her infinite eloquence, Audre Lorde expresses the depth of the challenge conscientious writers take on in "Poetry Is Not a Luxury":

> As we learn to bear the intimacy of scrutiny and to flourish within it, as we learn to use the products of that scrutiny for power within our living, those fears which rule our lives and form our silences begin to lose their control over us.
>
> For each of us as women, there is a dark place within, where hidden and growing our true spirit rises, "beautiful/and tough as chestnut/ stanchions against [y]our nightmare of weakness and of impotence."[1]

CHAPTER 1

Twentieth-Century Multicultural Women Writers of North America

Women's struggles for self-determination, survival, and self-respect are manifest in women's literature over the past century. The conclusions I draw from the works I have selected cannot possibly apply to all women writers or to all contexts. However, feminist configurations emerge from the collection of texts in which patterns of the development of feminist theory are evident. One obvious example of historical change is the increased (though still inadequate) availability of contemporary literary works by women of color, by openly lesbian women, and by women from lower economic class backgrounds. Also, the availability and acceptability of works of fiction *about* protagonists and characters from multicultural positions has grown, and traditional canonical imperatives that reinforce the seeming universality of white, male, and economically privileged perspectives are being severely challenged.

Even within women's writing, all serious attempts to theorize the evolution of the feminist movement to its present status require one to navigate the challenging course that connects women's struggles (once understood as universal) with the complex array of subjective positions now recognized as intersecting with women's struggles. I welcome the complexity of subjective positions presented in contemporary feminist discourse, and I hope that my observations will add some insights to the vast discussion and interchange taking place without my ever laying claim to the authority to encapsulate, define, or circumscribe the voices of the women writers to whom I refer.

In this selection of women's writing, some general themes arise that span generations and individual differences alike, and include rebellion against traditionally designated gender roles and the attempt to create a space in which women can act freely in the world. The groundwork for the feminism expressed by women writers in the late nineteenth and earlier twentieth centuries was laid by figures such as Elizabeth Cady Stanton, one of the original suffragists who held council in Seneca Falls in 1848 to seek inclusion in a male-centered and male-dominated society. The suffragists, sometimes referred to as first-wave feminists or liberal humanists, sought assimilation into the power structure through gaining the status of voting citizens rather than through social upheaval and the reconstruction of a new paradigm. They were predominantly white women who likened their cause to that of black Americans seeking the vote, but they were not unanimously supportive of African American rights. Elizabeth Cady Stanton, speaking to the New York State Legislature in 1854, stated that "we ask no better laws than you have made for yourselves. We need no other protection than that which your present laws secure to you."[1]

Inherent in this plea is the assumption that women have the right to assume self-consciously subjective identities. And yet the legal and cultural obstacles to obtaining equal status with men have not entirely disappeared even a century and a half later. The characters in the novels included in this study commonly experience isolation, self-hatred, and ostracization from the professional male-dominated public world. In the earlier works from the first part of the twentieth century, isolation from the male/public world often takes the form of confinement to the domestic sphere. In later works, women characters are presented as being held back from attaining social and economic status normally granted through male privilege, and sometimes through white heterosexual privilege as well, even in those cases where women are part of the salaried work force.

Judith Butler's discussion in *Bodies That Matter* of psychoanalytic theory and its failure to acknowledge race, gender, class, and heterosexism and the interlinking of each of these factors in the formation of subjectivity makes it clear that the neutral gender status aimed for in Cady Stanton's statement is already, in and of itself, a non-neutral category. "Neutral" subjectivity exists historically within the domain of a white male paradigm and is therefore unavailable to women because they are positioned as the other of the male subject. The centrality of such a subject relies on the existence of the other.[2]

The first women writers I consider are European Americans of the early twentieth century. They are educated and economically privileged, as the fact that they had the opportunity to write and publish works at all demonstrates. In addition, their status may well have given them an anomalous degree of freedom and autonomy. Many of their characters, however, are heavily burdened with non-subjective presence (a non-present presence), and live lives full of restrained misery and inner resistance to their circumstances. The writers in this group include Charlotte Perkins Gilman, Willa Cather, and Sarah Orne Jewett. Although I can only speculate on the effect the pervasive cultural acceptance of Freudian psychoanalysis at the turn of the twentieth century had on these writers in their articulations of gendered existence, its presence is undeniable.

In Charlotte Perkins Gilman's story, "The Yellow Wallpaper," the protagonist is a women living on her husband's estate, which is replete with servants, manicured flowerbeds, orchards, and elegant surroundings. The role she is called upon to play is that of his lovely, charming, presentable, and well-cared-for wife. He is a busy man who is often absent from home, and she is a dissatisfied, bored, secluded housewife whose discontent turns gradually pathological. Her inability to fulfill her wifely role is blamed entirely on her perceived shortcomings as a woman.

A psychoanalyst, in the vein of the times, insists that she refrain from manly pursuits, such as reading and writing, in order to avoid further straining her supposedly limited rational faculties. She is told to rest often, to entertain herself with light pursuits, and to take walks in the fresh afternoon air of the estate's extensive gardens. Rather than refreshing her intellect, these prescriptions stifle her. She most likely also internalizes self-blame for her predicament. As Judith Butler has pointed out, the superego of Freudian psychoanalysis, which is the controlling agent of the mind as well as the law, the censor, and the judge, is in fact white, male, and explicitly racist, sexist, and classist in origin. It is a social creation, an internalized external self-condemning gaze which Gilman describes as the effect of internal self-hatred, external monitoring, and punishment on women in "The Yellow Wallpaper."[3]

The protagonist descends with reader in tow into abject, utterly painful madness. It is as if life itself is forced from her. The tension of this piece for the reader revolves around the revelation partway through that there is no way out for this woman, and yet one continues reading. The hope of any possibility of escape lessens and lessens. In fact, madness becomes her escape—the only dismal possibility open to her. Eventually, she is confined in a room and the wallpaper comes alive to her. She begins living in the patterns, in which she sees hidden figures from another world, a world of freedom and movement she can never penetrate. In one sense, this is an analogy for women's relationship to male-centered subjectivity.

The reader is left with a hopeless sense of desolation and despair, wondering if, given the chance to live in the world as anything other than an attractive domestic mannequin, she might have found a more enlivening outlet for her energies. The only possible outcome for this novel is failure. There is no happy ending. Instead, an analysis of the deadly effects of the separation of womanhood from the subject-"neutral" position relegated to masculinity is offered as a critique rather than a remedy.

In two of Sarah Orne Jewett's short stories, a similar desperate state of affairs exists for the female characters. In "The Landscape Chamber," the exception is the narrator, who, as a traveler passing through, exhibits her chosen independence and freedom from the required gender decorum. She is not in any way entangled in the scene she encounters, or perhaps I should say she is able to escape relatively unscathed. Alone on horseback, journeying through the countryside, she is seeking diversion from ordinary life as unselfconsciously as any man might.

When her horse is temporarily incapacitated, she is forced to stop and spend the night on a dreary, decrepit farm that seems drained of vitality. The state of the farm is reflected in the person of the patriarch of the household—a miserly, ugly old man who is gray, lifeless, and severe—and his daughter, a grown woman whose persona seems mysteriously ghostlike and meek, as if her very spirit has been sapped by her father's domination. After a bland, unappealing meal, the narrator retires to a bedchamber and is startled by the old man's appearance. She feigns sleep as he stands by her bedside staring at her.

In the morning she leaves on her horse without looking back and tries to push the image of the imprisoned, wilted daughter from her mind. She does not rescue her; she disassociates herself from her. She puts as much distance as possible between herself and the silent despair emanating from the dominated woman.

I would like to suggest that the pull against which she is fighting is the recollection of the father's authority, which influences her own life in the form of a culturally created superego. Even as an independent woman, she may still harbor wishes to please the father (the law, patriarchy) rather than challenge gender norms as she does. The figure she identifies with deeply, and who therefore threatens her, is the daughter who has accepted her subservient role and has consequently gained the approval of the father: "Her eyes begged me entreatingly, 'Give him his own way'; her firm-set mouth signified her assent to the idea that I had no right to demand favors."[4] It is this subservience, which she sees as akin to death and the wasting away of joy in life, from which she is fleeing. She is fleeing from life as a woman in an overbearing patriarchal society.

Interestingly, Sarah Orne Jewett had the means to, and did in fact enact a certain degree of isolation from patriarchal, heterosexual norms. She is known to have never married—a man, that is. She lived for several decades with another woman in Boston and went alone on a writing retreat to the Maine coast a few months out of the year. And yet she did not write about openly lesbian characters. She wrote instead about the terrors of domination and how to avoid it through movement, through not allowing oneself to be pinned down.[5]

In a second short story, "The White Heron," a young girl named Sylvia nearly gives away the nesting location of a pair of rare white herons to a handsome young scientist out to collect bird carcasses for display when he pauses to stay at her grandmother's isolated homestead. Her naive excitement at the attention he lavon her nearly leads her to betray the birds she loves. The handsome bird collector, older and more experienced, knows this and plays on her growing need for his approval. In the scene where they first meet, an omniscient narrator informs the reader, "The enemy had discovered her, and called out in a very cheerful and persuasive tone."[6] He is conniving and ingratiating. Even her grandmother is fond of him. And yet he is after only one thing—those herons!

In the end, she leaves early in the morning for a remote and secret destination and climbs a tree from which she can see the distant shoreline. She gazes beyond her own domain. The exhilaration of her climb and the vast panorama that greets her brings about a profound sense of elation. In a tall tree, she sees the pair of white herons who are like old friends and, focusing on the male, she observes the love, loyalty, and tenderness of his attitude toward his mate. He also sees her. She imagines a kinship between them. Won over by this nobler presentation of masculinity, she rejects the weak, treacherous, selfish, and even malicious attempts by the young man to win her confidence through deception. She realizes that in reality he has nothing to offer her and that he is a menace to be avoided.

Interestingly, in all of the scenes in which the young girl is alone in nature, she is extraordinarily present in the narrative. She feels every nuance, every leaf turning, every breeze or drop of moisture. In social interactions, however, she is a silent onlooker, barely acknowledged by the young man until he realizes he can get something from her. She is a castoff from a large, poor family, taken in by the loving embrace of her grandmother and of nature.

The greatest force at work in both stories is a desire for freedom tempered by an unwillingness to completely let go of societal affirmation and interaction. Each has a hidden subtext of something like a call for feminist separatism. But in "The White Heron," more than in "The Landscape Chamber," there is a sense of hope and even a vision of another possible approach to relationships between the feminine and masculine as evidenced in the relationship between the male and female herons. Perhaps Sarah Orne Jewett envisions an equal society, even though these stories seem to be warning away from the traditional relationships men have to women, either as lovers or fathers, because of the inevitably dominant position of the male in the male-centered hegemonic cultural setting of the time.

In Willa Cather's novel *A Lost Lady*, we again see the specter of a restless vital woman confined to her household with little hope of escape. Mrs. Forrester, a character seen largely through the eyes of a young male narrator named Niel, leaves the life she has led as an attractive socialite in the west to settle down with an older, stable, loyal husband of some local prestige, Mr. Forrester, in the small town of Sweet Water on the western plains. She is bored and dissatisfied with her life, and as a partial remedy invites Niel in as their social companion in the evenings.

Niel is smitten with her, as are, seemingly, all of the men who make her acquaintance. She is beautiful and knows the social graces. The young man, who is in awe of her, gradually notices that her interest in her husband's welfare is superficial and merely correct. In fact, in a hidden arbor, Niel chances on a romantic encounter she has with a tall, dark, handsome visitor, which marks the beginning of his disillusionment with the object of his affection. As the novel unfolds, Mr. Forrester exhibits increasing signs of old age and infirmity and Mrs. Forrester's clandestine lover disappears. Lonely and helpless, she falls into a state of depression and alcoholism. Finally, with her husband's death, she falls into financial ruin. Under Niel's pitying gaze, she also engages in embarrassing debauchery with a no-account worthless local young man who is using her for his own gain, much as the male character in "The White Heron" attempts to use the little girl. The degenerate man who seduces her is the same character who, earlier in the novel, was viciously sadistic as a young boy to small animals, and terrorized the younger boys. Eventually, although Niel wants to rescue her, there is nothing he can do anymore.

One of the points that is evident throughout the telling of this story is the taken-for-granted fact that Mrs. Forrester has no control over her fate and is completely and helplessly given over to the only choice she is allowed to make in her life; that is, who will be her lover. Her husband and subsequent lovers seem arbitrarily to decide her fate. Her husband, whom she married for saving her life on a camping expedition, made a decision to isolate her in the small town of his childhood. He left her nearly penniless when he opted to pay off investors in a failed bank. Her extramarital lover might have carried her off—and been her escape—but he had other plans. Her last lover divested her of her final vestiges of wealth, land, and social prestige. She had no avenues of self-determination except to drink to ease her pain and entertain young men with parties in order to live vicariously through the freedom and vibrant possibilities they embodied. She herself had nothing but passion with no outlet, and good looks that led her not to her own subjective presence but merely to a tenuous connection to the subjectivity enjoyed by men.

So again, this tale, much like Charlotte Perkins Gilman's "The Yellow Wallpaper"and Sarah Orne Jewett's "The Landscape Chamber," seems merely to be a kind of eulogy decrying the fate of a woman who could not be rescued because there was no way out. We pity Mrs. Forrester perhaps, but leave it at that. What else could she have done under the circumstances anyway? However, there is a reading within the reading which provides a possible subcontext for this piece. What if Niel is not a man but instead a veiled woman?

Niel is, after all, presented as far more sensitive and caring than even the better men in the novel and as the antithesis of Ivy, the evil boy who later becomes the man who takes advantage of Mrs. Forrester's trust in him. When Ivy sadistically blinds a bird in front of a group of boys that includes Niel, Niel climbs a tree hoping to catch the bird and put it out of its misery:

> The woodpecker rose in the air with a whirling, corkscrew motion, darted to the right, struck a tree trunk to the left, and struck another. Up and down, backward and forward among the tangle of branches it flew, raking its feathers, falling and recovering itself. The boys stood watching it, indignant and uncomfortable, not knowing what to do....There was something wild and desperate about the way the darkened creature beat its wings in the branches, whirling in the sunlight and never seeing it, always thrusting its head up and shaking it, as does a bird when it is drinking.[7]

Niel fails in his attempt. He falls and breaks his arm instead. The bird, foreshadowing his relationship to Mrs. Forrester, is beyond his help. Because Mrs. Forrester does not see Niel as a man, he cannot save her from charming, seductive Frank Allister and conniving, devilish Ivy. Niel is a promising and faultless character. His youth makes him "not quite a man" in her eyes, but he adores her, understands her, and would care for her if only she would allow it. He is the superior choice. Instead, she falls for inferior models. If

Niel is indeed a stand-in figure for Willa Cather, it is interesting that although he loves Mrs. Forrester, he sees her as hopelessly in need of a man, of him.

Willa Cather was a friend of Sarah Orne Jewett who, like her, lived out her adult life in close, consensual, long-term relationships with women. In fact, in her earlier years she dressed as a man and called herself Will. In a piece entitled "Tommy, the Unsentimental," Willa Cather reveals partway through that "Needless to say, Tommy was not a boy, although her keen gray eyes and wide forehead were scarcely girlish, and she had the lank figure of an active half-grown lad."[8] The latter part of this description fits Niel to a tee. He is a near-man who looks on at the heterosexual marriage of the Forresters but is not himself yet a contender in their arena. He is described at nineteen as "a tall, straight, deliberate boy. His features were clear cut, his gray eyes, so dark that they looked black under his long lashes, rather moody and challenging."[9]

Knowing of Niel's admiration for and understanding of Mrs. Forrester, as well as his deep sympathy, even empathy, for her predicament, it is not impossible to imagine Niel as a stand-in for a masculine-identified female lover for Mrs. Forrester. Indeed, the descriptions Niel offers of her idealized femininity are not far off from the description of the woman Tommy finally brings home from the east, "a dainty, white, languid bit of a thing, who used violet perfumes and carried a sunshade."[10]

I would like to offer the interpretation that there is a veiled possibility of release being offered here. By assuming a masculine or subjective stance, both Sarah Orne Jewett and Willa Cather position themselves outside the women-as-absence and women-as-submissive and the passive framework they see as inevitable in the heterosexual paradigm of the period and in the economic/racial context in which they wrote. All three authors, including Charlotte Perkins Gilman, warn women to steer clear of scenarios in which they are supposed to be cared for in luxury and placed upon a pedestal, but instead turn to stone like the pedestal itself. The only glimmer of hope, not fully articulated, is the possibility of stepping outside the context.

Sarah Orne Jewett presents neutral characters who seem to live outside ordinary social contexts and therefore are untouched by the rigid strictures of prevalent gender norms. Willa Cather presents male/female figures who themselves are not confined by constricted female roles and who, at least potentially, treat their female lovers with a tenderness and kindness she sees as sorely lacking in male-female relationships rooted soundly in notions of difference, distance, and domination. In the character of Niel she expresses an admiring masculine gaze that disavows any possibility of emulating the indifference, cruelty, arrogance, and disdain of the rival men in the story. He does not want to use her, although perhaps he does want to own her; even he is not neutral. He does not easily part with the woman he so admires; instead, with reluctance and sadness, he realizes that he cannot save her.

The feminist message of the stories, without the veiled context of lesbian separatism, is somewhat dismal. The message is that there is a need for change because the role of women as narrowly defined within rigid patriarchy is untenable. If there is anything positive in these revelations, it is the emergence of a voice of dissent and disillusionment in contrast to the prevailing attitude of public acquiescence. To speak at all about the hidden realities behind genteel images of domestic harmony and complacent wives is to disrupt the dominant structures of power, and inevitably, therefore, to spark revolution.

In the works of more recent and contemporary writers, feminism is conjoined with other considerations. I would like to apply Judith Butler's criticisms of feminist psychoanalytic theory to feminism in general in order to demonstrate at least one direction I believe contemporary feminism is taking. Butler criticizes feminist psychoanalytic theory for its attempt to control the domain of the subject by emphasizing masculine and feminine formations as the most fundamental and basic categories of difference. This outlook, she suggests, is rooted in the work of Lacan, who branched off from Freud's notion of the superego as a force that sets the norm and standards through which socially ideal femininity and masculinity are established to show that the structure of language itself dictates conformity to these categories. Butler points out that many feminists take the fact that any use of language carries with it shades of sexual categorizing to mean that this category is therefore more fundamental than other factors of identity, and thus mistakenly feel that they do not need to address issues of race, class, and so forth. They assume an essential subject who exists at a fundamental level beneath the layers of other differences. This leads to tacit acceptance of a white subject within feminist psychoanalytic discourse because this supposedly fundamental difference of gender stands in isolation, untouched by race.[11]

Butler strives to show not only different factors that constitute the subject but also the nature of the connectedness of these variables. In some places she speaks of intersections and in some cases she speaks of the inseparability and interconnectedness of the variables. In her view, no single variable, such as feminism, can be isolated, analyzed, and then added to the equation.

Various writers have represented the complexity of female subjectivity by exploring other marginalized aspects of the individual that limit her claim to fully realized subjective presence in legal and social terms. Alice Munro's *The Beggar Maid* presents an inner picture of the life of a character who would be marginalized in many canonical works. Although the protagonist, Rose, is white, she is poor, and for this reason she feels distant from her college classmates and experiences a disjointed relationship with her wealthy boyfriend. When she arrives at the college on scholarship, she is treated in a patronizing manner and is expected to be meekly grateful for the charity given her. The fact that her scholastic abilities have played a role in her attainment of a scholarship is overlooked by those who humiliate her in subtle ways.

Her relationship with her boyfriend, Patrick, is viewed by those around her as a lucky catch on her part. Everyone, including Patrick, assumes that she is as thrilled as can be. She has trouble, however, deciding what exactly she does feel about him. It is not passion, but she does like him, even though she feels he is weaker than she is in some essential way. She is more daring and forthright, less pretentious and socially inept than he is. And yet when she acknowledges to herself the limited possibilities she sees as available to her, she agrees to marry him.

It is evident that more than practical financial worries shape Rose's choice. She also feels in her connection to him a growing awareness of the privileges denied her as a single woman with limited income opportunities. In contrast, his life is an open field. The only way he could possibly avoid succeeding would be to actively renounce his status and family ties. This feeling is exacerbated by the foreboding presence of Dr. Henshaw, an elderly single academic matron who gives her a place to stay, and Rose seems resigned to solitude and the sacrifice of sensuality and spontaneity. She fears the possibilities that lie in wait for her if she doesn't marry. She cannot face the possibility of college if she says no to Patrick, she claims, because the other girls will taunt her. And yet, until this point in the story she has been largely impervious to their opinions. It seems that her presence in the world as a woman in relationship to a man casts her into competition for success in traditional female roles—that is, that she is a success if she can bag a successful man and a real loser if he gets away.

Rose is defiantly searching for her place as a woman in a professional educated world that is new to her. Her background did nothing to prepare her; this situation is in a sense analogous to that of many women in the period referred to (the 1950's, even though the story was written in 1977). Although Rose seems able to ignore the outer obstacles she faces, she must deal with her feelings about herself, her hidden fears, and her sense of inadequacy. In this story we can almost trace the growth of feminism from the liberal pragmatism that fought to be included in the political mainstream to the cultural activism that sought to empower women by helping them to see themselves as strong individuals able to achieve any goal. The step Rose takes in this story involves introspection—the acknowledgment of emotional states that indicate a gap between the lived ideal and the actual feelings of the person living out the role. Rose's dilemma is to find out how to live without living out a role, since even when she seemingly defies convention she finds herself gravitating toward the security of the known—that is, being taken care of by a man—or else submitting to other allotted roles/ professions for single women.

The next works of fiction play liberally with location, setting, and sometimes chronological order. These stories are in a sense less settled. Certainly they are less linear and, perhaps because of this, deal head-on with very specific moments of terror and pain. The writers include Margaret Atwood, Toni Morrison, and Anne-Marie MacDonald. In the first piece, *Cat's Eye*, by Margaret Atwood, we observe the world through a gaze that fluctuates between that of an adult woman reflecting back on the childhood that formed her as a woman and the viewpoint of that child. As a child she struggles with a sense of insecurity over not measuring up to a feminine ideal. She is raised in an unconventional academic nature-oriented family. In her early years they are on the road and everyone participates in her father's research in wooded areas. Her brother and she relate as people who have a common ground. Her mother wears pants. Gender doesn't seem like a big deal.

Then the family settles in Toronto. She is tormented by her female companions for being oblivious to feminine imperatives, and she feels like a freak and an outcast. Even her mother cannot comfort her. She becomes distanced from her brother, who succeeds because his originality and initiative reinforce his masculine presence in the eyes of teachers and friends. He is allowed to be unique, interesting, and intelligent, even to be willful. She, however, to survive, isolates herself from anyone who can place judgment on her, because just to live is to be defiant. She is not a stereotypical girl. She needs to feel her presence in the world as a conscious being, but that subjectivity is normally awarded to males.

As an adult artist, the act of expressing her pain and the difficulty of *being* as a woman create a new ground of subjectivity for her and perhaps a vindication of the fact that she did not conform overly well to feminine norms as a girl. This once-seeming weakness has become her strength. Perhaps this is a dilemma still faced by the adult artist in *Cat's Eye,* that she must sort out her presence in the world, for so much of her presence growing up as a woman was defensive, angry, and apologetic. As an adult she seems to feel that she cannot deny that painful past, even if she has survived it, without risking covering over the truth of her agonizing experience of femaleness in a male-centered world.

In Toni Morrison's *The Bluest Eye,* a young girl grows up with the outsider status of not only being a girl but also of being black and poor. She suffers daily torments, such as a white candy-store keeper not wanting to touch her hand, and develops a toughness on the playground to protect herself from boys who taunt her, including a wealthy black boy who kills a cat in front of her. She is the narrator who unveils and fits together the pieces of another young girl's descent into madness. The other young girl, brutally taunted and attacked by young male playmates, is later raped by her father. She is not someone who can articulate her situation, and she latches on to the fantasy that she has blue eyes to counterbalance the tragic isolation that surrounds her when people realize she is pregnant and that it is the result of incest. She wants acceptance and the most basic kindness, characterized by an absence of violence. She wants to be told she's pretty and lovable, not someone hateful and disgusting.

In this complex image we see a character who is to be pitied as a victim of circumstances and yet who could have been saved were our culture as a whole not so brutal in its insistence on normalizing—punishing a woman for not being a man, punishing an African American for not being white, punishing a poor person for not being able to get away with what a wealthy person can. This text can easily be read as a feminist text, but it is not primarily feminist, since each of these other issues is just as present in the narrative and just as significant in shaping the challenges faced by the main characters.

Fall on Your Knees, by Anne-Marie MacDonald, chronicles the lives of several generations of women and their fates at the hands of men. Issues of race and class abound throughout the novel. I will focus on the last section. The main character of this section is Kathleen Piper, the daughter of a poor Irish white man who eloped with a young wealthy Arabic woman he met on Cape Bretton Island. She grows up as the apple of her father's eye. She is beautiful and develops into a talented singer. As a child, her father lavishes love, affection, beautiful gifts, and clothes upon her in contrast to the disdainful and abusive way he treats her mother and sister. Her mother goes mad as a result of her father's violent disdain for her; however, Kathleen never realizes that she is a stand-in for her mother in her father's eyes. She is a splendid and perfect woman admired by many and is seen by her father as his creation and possession.

Eventually, as a young adult Kathleen is sent to New York City, where she experiences freedom she's never known before. While training in classical operatic singing, which she finds tedious, she becomes friendly with her piano accompanist, Rose Lacroix, who is female, poor, and African American. The two become lovers and cruise the jazz scene of Harlem in the 1940s. The accompanist dresses as a man. The father gets wind of the affair, is enraged, comes to collect his daughter, rapes her, and impregnates her. She dies in childbirth. Although this is just one strand of a complicated web that unfolds in the course of the story, it illustrates that power relations, which shape each person's responses and actions, are often the result of a choreographed, multifaceted, yet concrete and tangible set of cultural circumstances.

In the love affair between the singer and accompanist, the singer seems to have the upper hand because she appears to be white and wealthy, even though her mother is not white, and her seeming wealth is only due to sacrifices imposed on the rest of her family. In contrast, the accompanist's mother is a white prostitute, although Rose herself appears to be black. Her working-class background is evident to Kathleen from the start because her clothing is awkward—she wears dresses that don't fit quite right or don't match. (Of course, it turns out that this is also a marker of her male-identification, since she cuts a fine figure in a suit.) Kathleen feels quite superior at first with her fine clothes and features that are much admired by the dominant white male world.

Kathleen's sense of superiority is short-lived; when she sees Rose in a suit, the accompanist appears dashing and exciting. They fall in love, and Kathleen's culturally inscribed, paternally granted sense of her own importance begins to dissipate. However, any claim to self-esteem and self-autonomy is truly stripped from her when she is raped and taken home against her will by her father. Kathleen is not in control of her fate because her father is absolutely convinced that she must exist as the fulfillment of his vision rather than as herself. When he discovered that she had acted on her own life plans, he took back what he felt was justifiably his.

The next two examples are historical pieces written as personal narratives to bring to life an actual figure in history whose story was largely covered over in her lifetime. The first of these is *I, Tituba, Black Witch of Salem*, by Maryse Conde, which is written in the form of a memoir spanning from before her birth to after her death. Tituba was an enslaved person from the Caribbean who was brought to Salem by Puritans and found guilty of being a witch. There is only passing reference to her in historical records. Maryse Conde weaves together her loves, her trials, her enslavement, and her freedom with far-reaching social contexts. For example, Tituba's blackness is clearly, for the Puritans, the source of danger, darkness, and chaos. She also symbolizes all elements of corporeality, such as sensuality, attunement to nature, and feminine intuition. These associations are theirs, not Tituba's, and the narrative stays closely attuned to her viewpoint, shedding light on the depth of underlying racist assumptions that permeate our culture even today.

The second historical narrative piece is hard to characterize and fit into any category. Toni Morrison's *Beloved* looks back to resurrect the painful buried memories we as a nation carry of the suffering and dehumanizing atrocities of the past. Morrison carefully researched the lives of enslaved African Americans and discovered a newspaper article about a woman who escaped to freedom in the north and was recaptured. Rather than allow her children to return to slavery, she killed them. (This is not an isolated phenomenon, by the way. Chronicles and diaries of post-Columbus Caribbean history, for example, indicate that many of the Arawak people killed their children to prevent their suffering under slavery.)[12]

Toni Morrison brings this story to life in an interwoven tale told by many voices. In it she draws connections that reveal the cultural roots that created the system of enslavement and shape perceptions today of how hegemonic white America views African Americans and how African Americans view themselves. Like Maryse Conde, her project is to uncover and unbury the past. It is to bring up the discomfort, to call forth that which has been dismissed in canonical history books. It forces, urges, and coaxes us, as readers, to look at what we as a nation are afraid to see and at that which has been painstakingly covered over with vague references that generalize, distance, and dehumanize the real lives that were involved.

These authors recognize that fiction has far-reaching political implications. These histories are not sets of abstract facts about wars and national economies but are rather the experiences of individuals; vast and complicated stories begin to unfold, and these stories undermine the entrenched social hierarchies in place today. The position of women is included in these analyses, but it is not isolated from other factors, nor is it prioritized as more significant than race or class. The feminism presented in these works is integrated feminism. Feminist analysis of these texts must take place within the milieu of other social forces. One cannot dismiss the blackness of Morrison's main characters, such as Sethe, as irrelevant to their situations as women.

Personal narrative often chronicles the life of an individual and, in doing so, reveals the particular position of the writer. *Wild Meat and the*

Bully Burgers, by Lois-Ann Yamanaka, tells the story of a young woman growing up Japanese Hawaiian and the particular issues of location and estrangement she faces. As a Hawaiian, she is distant from the mainland, and as Japanese, she is distinguished from her haole, Chinese, and native Hawaiian classmates. She is also from a poor family. She deals with many issues of self-perception, from her connection to her Barbie dolls to trick-or-treating at wealthy white people's homes. The stories she tells have a sense of everydayness and, at the same time, they have a twist that defies one to read them as ordinary. The "ordinary" accouterments of American culture are oddly displaced in her world, not the other way around.

In *When I Was Puerto Rican*, by Esmeralda Santiago, a similar kind of displacement takes place when the young protagonist arrives in New York City to live. She is held back in school, although she is a very capable student. She is treated as mentally deficient because Spanish rather than English is her first language. She overcomes these obstacles through determination. In the welfare office, translating for her mother, she describes the following scene as inspiration for her own unyielding faith in herself:

> Once Mami punched a social worker who was rude to her.
> "They treat us like animals," she cried after she had been restrained. "Don't they care that we're human beings just like them?"[13]

She succeeds in school and eventually goes on to Harvard. In a public talk at Ithaca College, in Ithaca, New York several years ago, Esmeralda Santiago shared with the audience that her book is indeed a chronicle of her own life. She added details from the point at which the story left off, such as her time at Harvard, where even though she worked full time, she graduated second in her class. She would have been first, except for one poor grade. No matter what she did, she couldn't satisfy the professor. Not surprisingly, he was one of the co-authors of *The Bell Curve*.

One last book I would like to mention is *Stone Butch Blues*, by Leslie Feinberg, a groundbreaking novel that shares the struggles faced by a butch, lesbian, working-class, white woman from Buffalo, New York who reaches adulthood in the early 1960s. From childhood on she has an appearance that is ambiguously gendered, and she faces abuse from parents and peers and later faces devastating physical violence at the hands of adult men. Eventually, she begins taken hormones and has surgery. Her appearance becomes that of a man, and the violence recedes.

Later, however, she stops the hormones because she questions her own motivations for the change. She feels as if she has lost control of herself and has lost herself in her bid for cultural acceptance. Throughout this novel, the reader is aware of the severe punishments women face for stepping out of line, especially when their biological appearance or sexual preference is out of line. This work of fiction not only illustrates the complexity of the interplay of different social factors in an individual's life, it also raises questions of feminism, such as who is a woman, and what is the aim of the women's movement for those individuals who cannot be easily assimilated into dominant socially posited gender identities. Feinberg's character does not blend in with the flow of media-fed gender perceptions. She cannot be a feminist in simple or obvious terms, and she certainly cannot be the type of feminist who seeks only minor changes and revisions in definitions of women's roles. She is self-identified as a masculine woman who herself loves feminine women in a masculine way and thus seeks the seemingly contradictory goals of allowing the defining criteria of womanhood to expand while preserving an idealized, sentimental, almost nostalgic image of feminine existence as the object of adoration.

Feminist ideology has broadened and become more complex since Elizabeth Cady Stanton's call for equal rights for women in the 1840s. There is no doubt that a white, heterosexual educated woman has less of a gap to jump in order to be accepted in professional male-centered cultural circles than a woman of color, an overt lesbian, or a poor woman. The oppression Cady Stanton spoke of is real. It is not negated by the increasingly complex picture of women's subjectivities that unfolds in contemporary multicultural women's writing; the point she raised is expanded.

We can begin to see that not only do we need to call for legal equality for all people, we also need to examine the causes of racism, sexism, classism, homophobia, and other forms of discrimination. Understanding the processes by which the seemingly ingrained mechanisms of oppression have developed serves to undermine these weighty forces by shaking them from the fortress of permanence. Whether inadvertently or purposely, the works of these women writers serve to disrupt fixed ideas of normalcy.

Relationships between the genders based on supposedly natural dominance and privilege are called into question.

As a result, contemporary feminism is broad-based. Each individual voice presents part of the picture. Each voice is significant. Recognizing this, we, as readers, can begin to understand the significance of our own lives. When I taught a course entitled The Power of Personal Voice in Women's Writing, I focused a great deal on the personal narratives my students wrote. Their writing about their own lives was an integral part of the course, because every previously silenced voice that is heard empowers all of us by decentering the power structures that keep privilege in place.

We need to do more than merely try to find a place in the canon for women writers and writers marginalized by reasons of class, race, and gender orientation. As Charlotte Templin has pointed out, by simply using the word canon, we universalize. It is a word set in stone, carrying with it an image of historical transcendence. The works of the canon are sanctified as if they were never created but instead arose directly from a divine origin. Glorifying the verses of the canon implicitly reinforces the idea that there exists an apolitical, purely aesthetic standard for measuring artistic value.

Not only are the authors of texts traditionally canonized male and white (Templin cites examples such as D. H. Lawrence, Herman Melville, and T. S. Eliot), the subjects and perspectives present in their writing reflect privileged white male experiences and outlooks. By rejecting the practice of canonizing we call into question the central position of these texts and the ideologies their content promulgates. It is not a matter of questioning the literary value of such works; it is a matter of critiquing the term "literary value" itself.

The exclusionary effects of canonizing are far reaching. When texts are categorized in terms of importance and political significance, we must ask who the arbiters are. What criteria do they use, and what is their stake in the choices made? The messages of the women referred to in this paper speak to a need not just to open up the canon but to do away with the notion of a transcendent universally valued canon.[14]

One should not assume that multicultural women writers are merely fighting to be included in the boy's club of "legitimately" talented writers; their work creates a new genre of writing. This is not to say that I agree with the practice of tacking on their works in the last chapter of huge anthologies of American fiction, because in fact these authors transform the way the works of white, male, supposedly neutral authors who have preceded them are interpreted. They challenge the presumption of white male mainstream authors that they produce neutral art—art for art's sake. No literature, past or present, can be presumed to be politically neutral any longer.

This continuing disruption of the veneer of neutrality is accomplished by these authors not just because they are women, people of color, or because of other factors. Their writing is subversive and transformative because they look critically at their position in the world and actively challenge those who are in positions of authority that enable them to circumscribe the rights of others. This process was already at work in the writing of Gilman, Jewett, and Cather. At times the nuances of their challenges are veiled or hidden. They are not as directly confrontational to the process of privilege as more recent authors, such as Morrison, Santiago, Yamanaka, MacDonald, and Feinberg, who focus on a direct and unbridled critical examination not only of particular individuals but of the entire system and structure of oppression.

The link between all of these writers is the obvious call in their works for transformation of oppressive aspects of American society and redress of the inequities suffered by oppressed individuals within that structure. Their writing could never be termed neutral, because that term implies a condition of stasis, complacency, and relative comfort with the status quo. The villains of seemingly neutral writing are individuals. The villains of these works by revolutionary writers are not just individuals; the villains are the power structures that give absolute significance to the will of particular individuals, while stripping others of the power to determine the course of their own lives.

CHAPTER 2

Butch/Femme Relationships in Works of Fiction as a Challenge to Heterosexist Paradigms

Representations of butch/femme identities in contemporary literature can either reinforce or challenge hierarchical gender paradigms found in traditional heterosexual relationships. I use two recent novels about butch identity and several short story collections, poems, and essays on butch and femme identities as well as the work of several theorists to examine the recent resurgence and acceptance of butch/femme relationships as part of a new trend in feminist thinking that strongly supports the right of the individual to freely express their gender choices. I explore cases in which having the freedom of individual choice makes such a position liberating and instances in which that freedom willfully perpetuates culturally familiar misogynist attitudes.

One of the most basic assertions of contemporary feminism is that transgressions of gender norms play a multifaceted role in establishing powerful and subjectively present senses of identity for women. At times feminist goals tend to address masculinity solely in terms of power structures that delineate the boundaries of gender as taboos which women, as subjugated citizens, must not break. So what happens if masculinity is addressed simply as a biological fact? Does the whole picture change? More fundamentally, is it even possible to separate the biological/psychological state of manhood from the social conditioning that posits masculinity within our culture as a privileged and superior status in comparison to female existence? This is the question I bring to my examination of female-to-male transgendered literature from a feminist perspective. When writers address very specific experiences of transgendered and lesbian butch/femme existence, these identities apply to a limited population, and yet, paradoxically, they also sometimes offer insight into the complex process of building a ground for female subjectivity in a misogynist, heterosexist, male-privileged, male-dominated, and patriarchal cultural environment.

The centrally located subject position granted to white males in our society is not natural, nor does it transcend history by tracing its roots to some deeper origin. It is rooted in an imperialist, colonialist, and economically exploitive history that has involved enslavement of African Americans; genocide of vast numbers of Native Americans; class stratification that created enormous wealth for some and hardship, poverty, and starvation for others; and the positioning of the male as the master over the female and *his* children. These issues are interrelated. The positioning of African Americans, Native Americans, the poor, and women in general into abject, defective distortions of the real, perfect, and powerful white male is not accidental. The subjugation of "the other" actively maintains the supremacy of the privileged position. The notion that the social structure that has shaped our past and continues to shape our present is somehow inevitable and grounded in an eternal divine plan leads to the sense that reality is unalterable, a way of thinking that enables social hierarchies to remain entrenched.

Ingrained cultural stratifications reinforce a distinction between the powerful, active male role and the passive, subservient, and arguably absent role allotted to women. Subjectivity itself is posited as residing in masculine presence, which is to say that masculinity is granted the status of neutral consciousness. Within this pervasive outlook, male experience is human experience. According to Sandra Bem, the author of *The Lenses of Gender,* images of the feminine have been denigrated throughout western history by sexism, entrenched homophobia, and mandated heterosexist paradigms that reinforce bifurcated, traditional patterns of masculine/feminine behavior. She cites examples from the Bible to Plato to Freud (who assumed a universal scientific stance that could not account for his own culturally rooted presuppositions concerning gender) to modern-day misogynist and homophobic views that linger not only in the fields of psychology and philosophy but in political and social realms as well. Bem states that

> Androcentrism is the privileging of male experience and the "othering" of female experience; that is, males and male experience are treated as a neutral standard or norm for the culture or the species as a whole, and females and female experience are treated as a sex-specific deviation from that allegedly universal standard.[1]

The role of woman is consistently viewed as lesser, and somehow defective, in order to reinforce the sense of competence with which men are seen to naturally fulfill their dominant role. Homosexual orientation and transgendered identifications are commonly seen either as disorders or criminally deviant. It was not until 1973 that American psychiatrists removed homosexuality from the *Diagnostic and Statistical Manual of Mental Disorders (DSM)*.[2]

However, a new diagnosis appeared in the *DSM* in 1980: *ego-dystonic homosexuality*, which referred to a person who felt afflicted by homosexual arousal and lack of heterosexual arousal. This category of pathology was criticized as homophobic, and was removed from the *DSM* in 1986, but it remained in place in 1987 under the category of Sexual Disorders Not Otherwise Specified.[3]

Interestingly, theorist Kenneth Lewes has speculated that the woman-fearing, misogynist stance of early psychoanalytic theory was replaced by homophobic attitudes as feminism gained momentum and the legitimacy of women's demands for equal rights became more and more accepted. He postulates that the male-centeredness of Freudian therapists was maintained through diversion of wrath away from women and toward homosexual men. In either case, heterosexual male identity is made to seem superior when juxtaposed against those viewed as flawed. Lewes postulates that deviation from traditional heterosexual male identity was considered a pathology until recently, despite the influence of feminist analysts who reinterpreted and revised Freud's work in a more female-positive context.[4]

In August of 1997, the American Psychological Association (APA) passed a resolution declaring that "homosexuality is not a mental disorder." Finally the APA has acknowledged that "so-called reparative therapy" that engages in an attempt to "treat" or alter sexual orientation violates the rights of lesbian, gay, and bisexual clients.[5] Even so, transgendered identity is still widely diagnosed as "gender identity disorder," particularly in the case of children or adolescents.[6]

The current trend of recourse to biological essentialism in popular discussions of gender demonstrates a reinforcement of non-neutral, polarized gender-norms. Whether we speak of the book title that has now become a common sound bite, *Men Are from Mars, Women Are from Venus*, or of the Promise Keepers movement, which calls upon men to take back the *responsibilities* of their supposedly God-given position of domestic authority and the privilege such a position entails, the underlying argument remains the same: women cannot and should not access the domain of men, since male privilege is viewed as the inescapable outcome of men's superior nature. In this light, any desire on the part of a woman to access authority, social power, or autonomy proves that she is both misshapen and insufficient as a woman, and a threat to the social order, or so-called family values, and to the continued existence of a hierarchy established to ensure the preservation of a male social elite. Hence the demonization of feminists (Rush Limbaugh's "feminazis") and of poor single women with children on welfare. (Erroneously presented as predominantly African American and as increasing in number, single mothers receiving welfare are chastised for stepping outside the social order of wedlock and the legitimized role of mother as obedient and dependent wife.)

A summary description of ideal femininity within this social framework would include a self-effacing attitude, youthfulness, ready compliance to male authority, chastity, a neat appearance, non-assertiveness, a slender build, non-competitiveness, and non-violence. Similarly, the stereotype of a feminine woman as a media-driven consumer holds that she is also physical, sexy, likes to buy things, and is prone to wearing expensive (sometimes tasteful, sometimes revealing) clothes that accentuate an image of youth and slender, elegant beauty. As long as her existence is physical and irretrievably associated with procreation and lust, she may speak, but only to an audience understood as male and presumed to be neutral and universal, or to an audience of women consumers who wish to obtain a performer's or model's idealized, feminine perfection. Except in the isolated case where a pro-feminist woman is speaking to other women within the confines of women's space, she is performing for the subject. Women's space, likewise, is often made to seem mundane and superfluous by male-centered media images, as if it consists of wholly innocuous and irrelevant domestic interests or preoccupation with physical appearance. Our cultural ideal of the feminine is a woman who objectifies herself in her presentation of herself. She knows how to entice and seduce, and she plays on images of helplessness and compliance as erotic expressions of her sexual vulnerability. She is treated like a lady and is therefore rewarded when she calls forth a response in men to protect, guide, and dominate her.

Another significant factor that plays into our cultural ideal of the feminine is presented by bell hooks in her critique of the cultural icon Madonna's appropriation of exotic racialized "otherness" while maintaining white privilege. hooks states that in Hollywood's view, "only white skinned females could be viewed as innocent, virtuous, transcendent." And, she also succinctly states, "Madonna's mega-success is tied to her representation as a blond. By assuming the mantle of Marilyn Monroe, she publicly revealed her longing to leave behind the experience of her ethnic and bodily history to inhabit the cultural space of the white feminine ideal."[7] Apparently, then, the rewards of feminine privilege are granted more readily to white women, but with the pervasive, historically entrenched cultural understanding that they are willing to subsume their authority under that of a man. This privilege is reinforced by media images that honor white femininity, or its approximations, as the ideal. In the context of an objectifying gaze, however, such images can still assume derogatory and exploitive aspects.

The image that bell hooks presents shows the overlapping complexities that prevent concerns for women's rights from standing apart from other human rights concerns, such as the right to racial equality and respect. In the image Madonna presents, her "otherness" and estrangement from male subjectivity in the role of a feminine ideal does not overshadow her position as subject as a paradigmatic representation of whiteness, and yet her *otherness*, which is to say, her objectified non-presence as a woman, remains insurmountable. She remakes herself again and again to create the illusion that her persona is a matter of personal and continuous choice rather than a by-product of the male gaze. Whether or not Madonna succeeds in recreating herself and, even more important, whether lesbian femmes can succeed in creating autonomous identities within butch/femme dynamics are important questions; is it possible for women to free themselves of the othering power of the male gaze and trust that the butch gaze is truly woman-affirming?

In terms of gender-transgressive lesbian butch/femme identities, this raises the question of what the underlying motives are behind chosen self-representations that seem on the surface to mimic traditional polarized gender roles. My sense is that butch and femme identities are interrelated and carry at least the potential to affirm female subjectivity. A butch individual can achieve this aim through claiming, and perhaps appropriating, male-subjective territory as a woman. The femme achieves this aim through reappropriating female territory by redefining and reliving her feminine identity within a context that affirms her subjective presence and value as a woman. This is possible because the position of a butch is not that of a man in the terms of the dominant heteronormative culture. She does not necessarily enjoy male privilege in that cultural setting; in fact several literary accounts of butch existence point instead to a distinct disadvantage butch individuals face in terms of self-esteem and social status as the obvious lesbian in a homophobic society. As a result, at least in some cases, butch individuals do not identify as superior to femmes or as completely differentiated from them.

Judith Butler has stated that gender is an open field of possibility:

> If gender is constituted by identification and identification is invariably a fantasy within a fantasy, a double figuration, then gender is precisely the fantasy enacted by and through the corporeal styles that constitute bodily significations.[8]

She also states:

> If the inner truth of gender is a fabrication and if a true gender is a fantasy instituted and inscribed on the surface of bodies, then it seems that genders can be neither true nor false but are only produced as the truth effects of a discourse of primary and stable identity.[9]

In this sense, the drag enacted in the display of butch/femme identities is not "uncritical appropriation of sex role stereotyping from within the practice of heterosexuality," but instead involves parodying these roles, thereby critiquing and transforming them.[10] If in fact the entire contextual ground of gender presentations within butch/femme identities is necessarily understood as having been uprooted and transformed into the open terrain of fantasized identities, then the meaning of masculinity and femininity must also be transformed in this process. However, not every butch and femme is a cultural theorist. They may be equally as capable as their heterosexual counterparts of reinstating their perceived self-identities in terms of gender as fixed, natural, and even true. There is every reason to assume that a butch woman or a femme woman is capable of holding a profoundly misogynist belief system.

Even when we acknowledge that the motivating factors behind gender identity expression vary according to the unique circumstances and choices of each individual referred to, we cannot deny the existence of a cultural template for valuation of gender. The reemergence of acceptance of butch/femme representations among contemporary lesbians is occurring within a national political context of increasing pressures for women to relinquish the freedoms gained in previous feminist struggles and to return to crusty old patterns of male domination and clear-cut legal and practical distinctions between the genders. It could be that butch/femme self-presentations are gaining acceptance and popularity as an oppositional response to seemingly inescapable patronizing and demeaning readings of the feminine. The most favorable reading of this scenario would be that the femme mystique nevertheless involves the reappropriation of the feminine, and the butch mystique is a reworking of masculinity that heals it of its privilege and reinstates it.

Of course, the other obvious possibility is that the butch claim to masculinity is a blatant strategic move to gain male privilege and deny any connection to the loathsome image of the feminine as a secondary, imperfect, and subordinate gender. It could be read as an attempt to cleanse the self of femininity and therefore of victimized status. In this interpretation, the femme gains a sense of affirmation enacted by and through the butch, who takes on the role of presumed subjective presence that the femme vicariously grasps and has a tangible connection to, a condition otherwise wholly denied her in her stereotyped presence in traditional heterosexuality. Perhaps she also takes shelter in, or is reflected off of, butch identity, through being herself recognized as a subjective, possibly equal, presence by her butch partner. Likewise, the affirmation of her feminine exterior as adequate grants her a quasi-subjective status, in the sense that she is assured that she has attained the objective ideal of a woman who is always a turn-on, who exudes femininity and is responded to, and is therefore rewarded with recognition by the subject, the butch. In this last case, her status as woman is glorified and reinforced—much as it is in the historical pattern of heterosexuality—not as a true subject, but by her ability to approximate an ideal.

Any of these possibilities may come into play, if not in every butch/femme relationship, then at least within the spectrum of butch/femme relationships. Shifts in cultural configurations of gender dynamics for an isolated population that exists oppositionally within a larger, heterosexually normative context may occur rapidly and in an unhindered, uninhibited fashion in comparison to the slow-moving rate of the larger rule-encoded society, but to suggest that this movement is entirely disengaged from harmful power inequities and the denigration of the other entails an unjustified claim to innocence.

However, with some legitimacy, butch/femme relationships are often shaped in current pro–butch/femme discourse as having been repressed historically by heterosexist society and, more recently, by lesbian/feminist imperatives of the 1970s and 1980s that called for women to become separatists from all patriarchal structures and representations. According to Minnie Bruce Pratt, "We didn't want to be women as defined by the larger culture, so we had to get rid of femininity. We didn't want to be oppressed by men so we had to get rid of masculinity."[11] In *S/HE*, she shares how she recovered the loss of her femininity through her relationship to a butch woman. She also shares vivid images of sex and love in which she, as a woman, is a central figure, the feeler, an all-encompassing subject. Her status throws off balance the image of women as passive sexual partners and as mere objects of passion.

In a section of *S/HE* entitled "Fear," Pratt shares her feelings of concern for her own safety and that of her butch lover when they were separated while jogging in a New York City park overlooking the Statue of Liberty. In particular, she worried about her lover's vulnerability to hate crimes. But a man who slowed down as he rode by on a motorcycle terrified her as well. When she and her lover reunited she learned that her partner had feared for her as well because she was a woman alone. Both figures share a position of subordination enforced by the threat of violence. They are not allowed to be subjects freely moving in the world, and they live with the backdrop of potential animosity and the unceasing threat of annihilation from those who claim the exclusive privilege of subjectivity over the gender categories these two lovers inhabit—female and transgender.[12] This is not to say that all men, or all heterosexual men, are violent. Rather, the rationalization for violent attacks is often based in broad cultural biases that reinforce a sense of entitlement and righteousness in the offender, as, for example, in the case of Claudia Brenner's account of a shooting rampage on the Appalachian Trail that killed her female partner and left her own body riddled with nearly fatal bullet injuries.

Brenner states that although the police were horrified at the event, and in fact admired her for having the tenacity and clarity of mind to walk some miles out of the forest to get help, even this open-and-shut case was challenged by the defense lawyer, who claimed that two *lesbians* had provoked and taunted a poor hapless heterosexual man who was understandably stirred into such an uncontrollable sexual frenzy that he acted out with a shotgun. The implication was that lesbians (and women) are purely sexual beings and exist under that threat of the enacted impulses of the dominant male. What were two women doing alone in the woods anyway, right? Brenner responded by writing and speaking publicly about her experience to demonstrate the bias of the legal system against lesbians (and women) and to point out the dangers of homophobic masculinity. The man who shot her and her partner felt that his feelings of disdain, disgust, and violent arousal toward the two women were perfectly justified.[13]

In Minnie Bruce Pratt's account of her relationship in *S/HE*, the narrator and her partner find refuge in each other against an onslaught of dehumanizing and violent gestures from misogynists and homophobes. Remembering her previous marriage, she recounts, "In the summer, I stumbled and fell to the floor as my husband threw me out of our house."[14] In another scene that takes place in the essay "Jellyfish," she crosses a hotel lobby on the way to a gay dance with her lover and feels a hostile male gaze infiltrate her sense of joy in her own sensuality. Even as she is aware of "lace shimmering on her breast," she is aware of the glares of men she interprets as arising from jealousy that she exists as a woman for her lover's gaze, not theirs.[15]

The fear and shame associated with her femaleness under the male gaze is sharply contrasted with the welcome sense of vulnerability she feels in passionate experiences with her lover: experiences that seem to reinvent her as a woman. Her vulnerability with her lover, as well as her active role, seem to empower her with a sense of love for herself as a woman. In these examples, she illustrates the dilemma she faces in existing as a woman in a dominant culture that derides her femininity and waits to pounce on any expression of her feminine qualities by violently demanding submission as appeasement. Rather than close off the avenues of vulnerability, she chooses to express her beauty as a woman in a setting that is free of veiled threats. With her transgender lover she finds herself affirmed as precious and worthy, as a female human subject. She is able to inhabit a subject position specifically denied women in the broader cultural context by reinventing gender with her lover.

That her relationship to her lover involves choice rather than the entrapment of her culturally imposed alter identity is obvious, but not all butches share her lover's vision. In one scene, after being insulted at a public talk by a butch woman who says, "You're a femme? Where are your fingernails?" she is told by her lover, "That's the kind of remark you expect to hear from men. And what kind of butch are they anyway, to put down another woman?"[16] The sentiment expressed in this quote implies a sense of derision for androcentric misogyny, whether it is generated by straight men or butches indoctrinated by heterosexual values. The affirmation of a woman's identity as a feminine, sensual, physical, yet autonomous, thinking, feeling subject in these narratives is accomplished in the loving space created by two lovers, butch and femme, who are willing and eager to leave misogyny behind in a conscious and heartfelt effort. They are aware, however, that at least some butch-identified individuals do not share this aim.

An analogous quest for subjective presence in the butch/transgender narrative takes place in the novel *Stone Butch Blues*, but in this case it is for the right of an f-t-m butch-identified individual to exist in an openly hostile world. I should note that *Stone Butch Blues* author Leslie Feinberg and *S/HE* author Minnie Bruce Pratt are partners, and that the complementary pattern I see in these texts is likely not coincidental.[17] Narrated in the first person, *Stone Butch Blues* follows the life of Jess from a tormented childhood in which her ambiguous gender appearance makes her an object of harassment by peers and strangers alike. Her parents force her to enroll in charm school and confine her intermittently to a mental institution. In high school she is raped by male classmates on a football field. In adulthood, at the hands of police and other male criminals who wish to violently suppress her gender identity, she suffers numerous counts of physical abuse and sexual violence. The narrator makes it clear that the constant onslaught of brutality and the never-ending threat of violence faced by Jess is a common challenge faced by other transgendered individuals, not only in the 1950s setting in which the book begins, but today as well. This conclusion is reinforced by Riki Anne Wilchins in her book entitled *Read My Lips*. In an informal poll taken at a transgender gathering in protest to perceived exclusion from the Michigan Women's Festival, she/he notes the following responses among twelve people: five incested, nine sexually abused as a child, twelve physically abused or beaten (as child or adult), six raped, two shot, three stabbed, and six arrested. Also, one person reported being burned, and one was horsewhipped.[18]

The violent scenes Jess describes carry with them a horrifying sense of erasure, a veil of invisibility with which her attackers attempt to cut her off from humanity. As Judith Halberstam states in her article "Between Butches,"

> Feinberg makes her readers aware over and over that the butch life is not simply heroism, motorbikes, suits, jeans and femme companionship; it is also defeat, poverty, violence, loneliness and the blues. The butches are shut down and closed off, left out and inappropriate.[19]

That erasure is enacted by Jess's abusers. Against this backdrop of never-ending terror, we hear the voice of the narrator, which, by speaking at all, by existing at all, by not being swallowed up in self-defeat, is defiant. This voice is ignored by the indifferent thugs who degrade and violate her, among whom are neighborhood boys, high school football players and their coach, policemen, random rednecks, thieves on a subway platform, and others.

In contrast, the narrator's affirmation of subjectivity, like a whispered voice that reaches across an abyss, stands forth with frightening and transformative strength. It speaks of the courage to stand alone and to realize in doing so that one is not alone but rather is surrounded by the force of all others who are rendered voiceless in patriarchal discourse.

And yet it is not a story of a battle won, except in the bare fact of survival itself, which under the circumstances is a kind of victory. This is evident in the conflicting emotions the novel's main character feels when she makes a decision to change her body hormonally and surgically to that of a man. She moves from being a butch-identified lesbian lover, emotionally supported only by her femme partner, to being a man. Rejected by her lover in the course of this transition, she gains public acceptance. Jess relates, "My beard grew in full of color: blond streaked with red, brown and white. In the open fields of life, my beard was a bush to hide behind."[20] The threat of violent suppression in a straight society from which Jess had always been estranged abates due to her new identity, but still a sense of isolation lingers. Desperation gives way to resignation. Her/his sense of isolation seems on the surface to be less extreme as a man. Women openly flirt with him and a male coworker befriends him, but she/he holds back from revealing too much of herself to his probing questions about her/his life, questions which might give away her/his past.

With the disappearance of his apparent gender ambiguity, Jess's confrontations with overtly violent attackers lessons, but Jess seems to develop a sense of estrangement even from her/himself in the sense that the person now recognized by the straight community around her/him doesn't correspond to the complexity of who she/he is. In one striking example, she/he makes love to a woman (Annie) without ever revealing that she has not always been a man, and pulls it off (rather remarkably I might add). She/he later finds her/himself attending a wedding with the same woman. The wedding in this case is an inescapably profound cultural signifier for naturalized heterosexual male/female binary roles and distinctions.

It is there, noticing a gay male relative, that Annie breaks the bond Jess and she have developed as new lovers:

> "Who let that queer in here?" Annie hissed.
> "Is he really gay?" I asked her.
> "You bet. Probably fuckin' all the children in the family."
> "Jeez Annie." My blood ran cold.[21]

The necessary lie cannot go on unless Jess completely suppresses her identity and denies her subjective presence in the world as a woman/man. To rid her/himself of the self-effacement and self-hatred of a gender corollary to internalized racism, Jess stops taking hormones and returns to a gender appearance that is butch/ambiguous. The reasons Jess gives for the choice include a sense of isolation and loss of connection to self-identity and the feeling that her original decision was made merely to mitigate the violence by appeasing her attackers. It is an act of affirming an in-between status that is unrecognized as legitimate by heterosexualized, bifurcated gender norms. It should be noted, however, that many contemporary transgendered individuals who have altered their bodies surgically and hormonally are quite open and out about the fact and are in no way striving to hide their transgendered status through conformity to heterosexual gender patterns.

Jess feels invisible as a man, but it is also important to note that until recently the female-to-male transgendered person has also been largely invisible in transsexual discourse. The particular situation faced by Jess has a different character than that faced by transgendered male-to-females. Whereas a m-to-f might be the object of rage and violence, it would be for giving up and therefore denigrating the position of male privilege in the eyes of his attackers. In contrast, a figure such as Jess, if visible and recognized, would be viewed as a usurper of gender privilege and as competition for feminine desire. In the psychological fields, which long pathologized m-t-f transgender identity, a figure such as Jess is not even recognized. Terms such as penis envy are used as examples by cultural theorist Marjorie Garber to demonstrate this institutional bias. In pointing out the centeredness of masculinity in psychological discourse on transgendered issues, she speculates that while it is considered normal for a man to want to be a man, it is also considered normal for a woman to envy the position of manhood. She also observes that the term transsexual has commonly been applied strictly to men. Subjectivity is seen as residing in the male, and thus the male, even when he gives up the position of manhood, is viewed by the medical establishment as still retaining male subjectivity.[22]

Nonetheless, Leslie Feinberg has positioned herself as an advocate for the rights of all transgendered individuals, as is made clear in her later theoretical text *Transgender Warriors*. *Stone Butch Blues* ends, in fact, with a badly beaten Jess suffering from a broken jaw and unable to receive follow-up medical attention when the attending physician discovers that she is not a man. She/he takes shelter with a transgendered m-t-f neighbor who nurses and cares for her and eventually becomes her lover. The profound empathy of the neighbor speaks of solidarity and familiarity with violent hatred and abuse.

A way of explaining the violence described in *Stone Butch Blues*, for indeed the novel challenges us as readers to ask why it occurs, is Judith Butler's observation that gender is performative. If gender is in fact constructed in the moment of performance, or parody, it takes on a transparent hue and in so doing reveals that cultural training itself is no more solid than a fantasy given the weight of cultural habituation. In this context, gender is the stuff that dreams are made of, which can be a threatening concept to a man who wants to know that he is a man and has seemingly legitimate access to his position of privilege as a man.

And we must remember, as always, that gender is not neutral. The image that comes to mind in cases of physical assault of either male-to-females or female-to-males is, in both cases, violence at the hands of angry males. In the case of Jess, it seems to be as much because she "doesn't know her place" and has jumped gender boundaries as because of the fact that her existence dissolves the boundaries that hold in place not only a male/female power hierarchy, reinforced by a continuous threat of violence, but all other supremacist hierarchies as well.

That Jess survives these onslaughts and finds a way to tell the story is heroic. The brutal exterior environment in which the events unfold is oddly distanced from the interiority and strong sense of introspection on the part of the narrator. Inside this harrowing tale of sickening violence and despair, an inner force of light and hope sometimes emerges, although it is accompanied by a kind of emptiness as well. In the scenes of domestic love in particular there is a sense of glowing comfort, of harmony and appreciation on the part of Jess for a transformative, affirmative embrace by loving arms.

In fact, the narratives of the scenes of loving are strikingly intimate and gentle, just as they are in *S/HE*. The scenes move with the weight of past pain carried into the openness of the present moment's soft and sensual encounter. The strike of a fist or raping member is juxtaposed in this narrative against the loving attention of Jess as a butch lover to her lover's needs and responses. It is a way of saying that in the sexual arena all that feeling can come out—all that pain we carry—and we, and our sense of ourselves, are transformed in a space of trust and unfolding. This is as true for the battered femininity of the femme caught in a male-centered cultural gaze as it is for the culturally annihilated subjectivity of the masculine presence of a butch woman.

Jess, as the reader is informed, is stone butch. So in unfolding her lover's anguish and passion, the language of their love clearly indicates that her lovemaking is distinguished from that of a man. In more than one instance, her lovers state that a man has never been so attentive. Annie says, "I never met a guy who wasn't afraid of a little bit of woman's blood. But you know what's weirdest about you?... You take your time you know. It's like you got a brain in your dick instead of a dick for a brain."[23] Feinberg makes it clear that the focus of Jess's lovemaking is on the experience of the femme lover and that this is the source of the intimacy of the passages, that in that moment of vulnerability and openness the touch is empathetic. Both women, butch and femme, and even f-to-m and femme, share an understanding of the way the brutality inherent in a relationship in which there is no balance of power between men and women has closed something down and that something can open up in this other created space. Butch/femme identities offer to contemporary lesbians the possibility of reclaiming the beauty of masculine/feminine energies meeting without the imbalance in power relations that demands an annihilation of everything feminine.

It is in this moment, in a space of insulation from the latent brutality lying in wait to destroy the access of a marginalized subject's claim to embodied, full existence, that both femme and butch share self-affirmation and affirmation of each other. Two subjects that have existed previously only in opposition to dominant discourse exist with the support of another gaze. And this self-affirmation, which occurrs at the meeting point of desire, at the gap that is closed between the actor and the acted upon, is an act of the utmost subversion. Here, at the moment that subjectivity is claimed and affirmed by another, a new paradigm comes into being.

This is true for both figures. The femme individual is accustomed to having her subjective presence purposely denied in current traditional heterosexual cultural contexts that represent woman as the absent other of manhood and the mere object of desire in love, even to the extent that the existence of her role except as servant and pleasurer is denied. Power is eroticized by the overpowering male subject in such a case, in a solipsistic, masturbatory fantasy made reality in which "the other" bends to the master's will. Love in such a context can never be the meeting of two individuals, and so it is worth exploring the possibility that butch/femme relationships, in some cases, can offer insights into what a meeting of equals, equals who are distinctly situated from each other, might look like.

The butch figure in this context is also in a subversive position in relation to the dominant paradigm because she is claiming a transformed male subjectivity as her own. If she is dwelling in a space of subjectivity with the underlying intuitive cultural awareness that her subjectivity is associated with her maleness, even granted her by her maleness, and yet she chooses to affirm the subjectivity of her femme lover (not to mention her own femaleness) by recognizing and prioritizing her presence and pleasure, then she is transforming the banal old script of lovemaking as the conquering of new territory and "scoring" into the erotic, which Audre Lorde defines as "born of Chaos, and personifying creative power and harmony… an assertion of the life-force of women; of that creative energy empowered, the knowledge and use of which we are now reclaiming in our language, our history, our dancing, our loving, our working, our lives."[24] Leslie Feinberg's character Jess transforms lovemaking from a template for colonization and imperialism into an act of communication between two distinct beings.

Together, two such lovers who overthrow the power structures that impede them find a fuller, richer experience of their own sense of self-existence. Their experience, however, is individual and does not speak for the experience of all butches and femmes. It may be true that the particular worldviews of Minnie Bruce Pratt and Leslie Feinberg are inextricably linked with their life experiences as a self-proclaimed butch and femme, but this does not mean that the philosophy of every butch and femme is based on the need for respect of gender choices/expressions and the fluidity of gender.

Leslie Feinberg's *Stone Butch Blues*, as well as her later work *Transgender Warriors* (which documents transgender oppression and activism), express a commitment to public activism that opposes classism, racism, sexism, and other forms of oppression that includes but is not limited to transgender oppression. *Stone Butch Blues* presents a socialist interpretation of the hierarchies at the root of the violence, hatred, and economic oppression that various characters—gay, lesbian, straight, and transgendered—face in a working-class setting in Buffalo, New York and later in New York City. Minnie Bruce Pratt likewise raises similar issues of sexism and racial exclusion in *S/HE*.

In stark contrast, Frankie Hucklenbroich's *A Crystal Diary* recounts the tale of a butch individual's life that does little to enhance the notion that butch/femme relationships offer a positive agenda for social change. At best, Nikki, the main character, can be read as a victim of circumstances, a drug-abusing outcast who can't seem to find work except in a criminal vein (she runs a house for prostitutes), but she *can* pick up women. She is a handsome butch whose story spans decades. As the novel progresses, it becomes evident that she despises women. She is proud of her lovemaking abilities, but thinks nothing of convincing a girlfriend to turn tricks to support her. Nikki is mean and dangerous. She knows that this touches off some attraction in certain femme women, and she draws them in like a flame draws in moths.

The unapologetic and revealing tone of this novel is in a sense refreshing. There seems to be no attempt to artificially turn the character into a morally reflective person. There is no apology, but rather a portrait of social forces and an individual acting out a dark tale of the effects of self-hatred, which unfortunately spills out in violent disrespect for others as well. Most readers, I imagine, can relate on some level to the dark apathy of the novel's poignant moments—even the raw, almost anonymous sexuality—because numb dehumanizing apathy is a part of our times, whether or not we endorse such feelings. The author shows us that we live in a post-industrial wasteland that shapes our estimates of human value. Rather than resisting the coldness and degrading aspects of this cultural landscape, the narrator and the main character dive in and experience the life of seedy bars, dark alleys, and restless poverty.

Unlike Leslie Feinberg's character Jess, who experiences similar depths of misery, Nikki does not fight back and she does not even despair. She survives. She gets what she can. In the throes of drug addiction she states, "If I had to choose between a good rush and almost anything else I'd be tying off my arm without a thought. I know people who've been doing crystal for years. I never met anybody who quit."[25]

Her attitude toward women is one of stark indifference and disdain. When she shares "The Code of the Stone Butch," one almost pictures the secret meeting in a smoky, dimly lit bar during the off hours of an underground butch gang poised to usurp the domain of male dominance and take over the world at the expense of women:

> Thou shalt always leave a woman's work undone, neither shalt thou cook nor make beds nor sew nor do any grocery shopping. Thou shalt, however, change tires, take out garbage, mow incidental lawns, and carry all heavy stuff from the car to the house. When living with someone, thou shalt handle any money which cometh into the pad, neither shalt thou be compelled to give an accounting therefor. Thou shalt not wear skirt or dress unless it be under duress vile, such as thy mother's birthday party or thy kid sister's wedding. Thou shalt demand fidelity from thy femme(s), even while thou fuckest at every opportunity. Then shalt thou be covered with honor and glory amongst all the butches of the land.[26]

In this parodic presentation of the butch code it is difficult to see anything other than gender polarities, fixed identities, and hierarchies. Hucklenbroich's character Nikki demands an almost exaggerated picture of culturally allotted male privilege. To engage in a deconstruction of this short poem as misogynist would seem almost trite. It is misogynist and it aims to be misogynist, and Nikki apparently hooks a lot of babes with her "no apologies" attitude. Even so, one could argue that displacement alone disrupts the entrenched hierarchies; she is, after all, a woman. Women who give in to her demands shift the focus of their ingrained tendencies to give way and give in from men to butches, and no doubt this giving in is eroticized. Such a line of argument would be similar to that used to explain the practice of lesbian S&M in its recent bid for legitimization within feminist-lesbian discourse, and in fact Nikki finally discovers S&M at the end of the book and finds sensuality unleashed in the act.

Feinberg, Pratt, and Hucklenbroich each portray transgender and butch-femme relationships through a slightly different lens. Feinberg offers the transgender butch whose fidelity, compassion, and courage point toward a progressive reading of gender-transgressive relationships between women. Both *Stone Butch Blues* and *Transgender Warriors* call for greater social recognition of the fluidity of gender identities and for the right of all individuals to live and love as they choose. Pratt's *S/HE* highlights the various types of internalized oppression within butch/femme relationships. Her work urges feminists to make room for political coalitions with women regardless of gender identity, and she unmasks the damaging stereotypes that label groups of gender transgressors as inferior. Hucklenbroich's *A Crystal Diary*, although more descriptive than theoretical, defends the stone butch as a sexual being and raises interesting questions about the sexual dynamics between butches and their partners.

Butch or femme identity in and of itself does not necessarily imply an interest in transformative humanitarian goals, but that does not mean that such identities replicate or reinforce oppressive attitudes toward women and other stigmatized groups. In fact, the struggle for the rights of those engaged in butch/femme relationships to represent themselves as gendered beings is part of the same battle for human rights that the feminist, lesbian, and civil rights movements have been fighting for decades in this country.

CHAPTER 3

Progressive Confrontation

This essay explores the cultural reverberations of works by contemporary lesbian feminists who openly flaunt their resistance to traditional feminine formations within the heterosexual patriarchal white context of broad-based societal norms. The feminism of this group of women is based on the idea that while trying to raise the status of women on a national level, the women's movement (taken perhaps mistakenly as a monolithic whole) strove to empower women through mainstream images that excluded alternative forms of expression.

Today's feminist movement is characterized at least as much by nihilism and hopeless indifference as it is by the moderate progress it has made in job and educational opportunities for women. In a sense, the progress serves to highlight how far there is yet to go and the daunting obstacles to fundamental changes in the perception of women as flawed, inferior, and less important and exciting than men. One could say that today's feminism is characterized by throwing in the towel, by saying that the society as a whole is not changing fast enough—in fact it is growing more conservative. Women's bodies are the site of one of the main battles in contemporary society. Women's access to abortion is threatened in the United States, single mothers and poor women who receive public assistance are demonized, and middle-class women feel great pressure to present themselves as sexually passive good mothers. Women who live outside this narrow framework of possibility, whether by choice or circumstance, threaten the status quo.

Feminism is not, and perhaps never has been, a single movement. The needs and concerns of feminists are not universal, and those groups who feel particularly excluded when political expediency motivates feminist/lesbian organizational decisions on a national level are voicing their concerns. Feminism and lesbian feminism as movements are being held accountable for omissions. The most visible members and leaders of early feminist movements participated in exclusionary practices by assuming that all women should assimilate the versions of womanhood feminist leaders deemed acceptable.

Audre Lorde castigates this mindset in her essay "The Master's Tools Will Never Dismantle the Master's House." She criticizes the thinking that relegated her participation in a 1979 conference on feminism to a panel designed to explore "the role of difference in the lives of American women: difference of race, class, sexuality and age." Her identity as a black lesbian was reduced to the category of "other," as if "lesbian and black women have nothing to say about existentialism, the erotic, women's culture and silence, developing feminist theory, or heterosexuality and power."[1]

Audre Lorde argued that differences between women should be seen as openings into productive communication and creativity. She called on the feminist movement to appreciate rather than fear difference and to consider the viability of a common ground of community based on interdependence. She called for feminists to move beyond tolerance of difference; that attitude already assumes the construction of a central dominant position that "tolerates" the presence of outsiders and expendable, silenced others.[2]

For some people, the Michigan Womyn's Music Festival represents a meeting ground for feminist women that creates an oasis outside dominant culture. Many see it as a microcosm of a greater national coalition of diverse feminist communities. Its detractors, a group of transgendered and butch/femme individuals including Riki Ann Wilchins and Leslie Feinberg, feel excluded from the festival and view it as an exclusive party to which only androgynous, narrow-minded women who accept old-school feminist definitions of lesbian relationships are invited.

When I first read of the exclusion of transgendered individuals from the festival, I was quite surprised given that the ideology of the festival has always been characterized by open-mindedness and acceptance of difference—perhaps even an exaggerated respect for different viewpoints and an insistence that those viewpoints be heard. Thus, the festival organizers have made numerous rules of conduct designed to accommodate each attendee's needs. For example, camping areas, and even seating for performances, are rigidly divided into numerous subdivisions of smoking, nonsmoking, drinking, alcohol-free, drinking but not smoking, vegetarian but tolerant of others, in bed by ten, in bed but awake all night with whomever, and on and on. The organizers strive painstakingly to give everyone their space and to make sure that each space does not intrude on other spaces. This is the setting in which differing philosophies regarding feminism, freedom, and sensuality meet. It is meant to provide a haven for women—a women-only space—and to create a physical boundary through which the patriarchy is not allowed to intrude for a few days. Men are not allowed to attend. The premise behind this rule seems obvious—that women act differently in the presence of men because they have been acculturated to defer to men and to hold back their own feelings and expressions. It is the same reasoning used by Mary Daly, who resigned in 1999 from her position teaching women's studies at Harvard after two male students sued to demand the right to attend her women-only classes. Women don't do many things in front of men that they feel free to do in a woman-only space; dress topless, for example.

The rules excluding males from the Michigan Womyn's Music Festival may be unfair to those who live on the margins of gender, whose identity is devalued and often unrecognized by the dominant culture. Many transgendered individuals have complained of not feeling welcome at the festival, although they report that they do feel included at queer community events. But in all fairness, it is also important to remember that women rarely have the freedom in our society to feel unselfconscious and uninhibited about their bodies. The festival is a rare space for women to experience such freedom. At the recent Woodstock commemorative festival in July 1999, which was meant to embody the open-minded free-love philosophy of the 1960s, there were several reported cases of sexual harassment and derogatory and suggestive remarks made to women, even by male police officers. Some male attendees at Woodstock read the behavior of women who felt free about their bodies in front of men as a licentious invitation. The threat of violence was in the air, and in fact some women were raped. In day-to-day life women guard themselves and are forced to monitor closely the line between sensual expression and dangerous exposure. The Michigan Womyn's Music Festival creates a safe space for women, and hopes to create room within that space for free expression.

I recently interviewed two women who regularly attend the Michigan Womyn's Music Festival and discussed with them the ways in which the organizers of the festival are dealing with possible conflicts between feminist goals and the need to recognize individuality and the right to free expression. Held every year for one week in August, the Festival regularly attracts 5,000 to 7,000 women. Although even this large gathering cannot encapsulate the diversity of contemporary feminisms, it is a place where women can communicate with each other about their lives and goals. Lynn, a five-year veteran of the crew, a group of between 400 and 500 women who facilitate the Festival, noted that the shape of the Festival was changing rapidly in the 1990s. She and her partner Ann noticed several controversies that arose during those years, but she also added that the controversies were small ripples that were addressed only by those people who were interested in or felt impacted by contested decisions.

One controversy involved the need to welcome and include women of color at the festival. Ann described the attendees as mostly white, middle-class women with money who are able to make the time to come. They tend to have feminist and lesbian ideals. But the group is not homogeneous. Many young, old, disabled, and international people attend. An organizational decision was made to officially create a workshop space for women of color as well as a "sanctuary tent." This was an attempt, I assume, to acknowledge difference and to deal with racist forces, which, like sexist forces, extend far beyond the confines of the camp. It was a gesture that was intended to give women of color the opportunity to feel unguarded, unobstructed, and unselfconscious as they expressed themselves.

Another recent controversy involved child care. As a growing number of lesbians have had or adopted children, this issue has become more significant. The question of what to do with male children in women-only space has emerged, a question that many lesbian separatist communities have had to deal with in the past. The official cut-off age for boys is twelve. The boundary between male gender and patriarchal forces becomes blurred in this instance, but the decision at the festival was likely made to eliminate the possibility of a male sexual gaze that would carry with it associations of a predatory inhibiting force. Workshops have also been created to answer questions about how to empower female children.

Unofficially, one of the more amusing controversies involved the "Bordello Incident," in which several members of the long-term crew partitioned off one of the buses one evening before the Festival actually began and several women charged for sexual labor. Lynn says that she heard about it secondhand and that it didn't cause much of a stir. Some of the women involved were professional sex workers. Some, in the spirit of the Festival, accepted barter in place of cash. Their presence for women only apparently carried a different meaning than it would have elsewhere and so did not reinforce an attitude that would equate sexual expression in women with an orchestrated submission to masculine desire or a sublimation of women's needs to those of men.

The largest issue that Lynn remembers, overshadowing all of the previous topics, is the debate over S&M sex. Sometime around 1990, leaflets were dropped by aircraft over the festival grounds supporting S&M practices. During that festival, when the issue was hot, many women openly engaged in S&M sex, wore collars, chains, or leather, and engaged in dominant/submissive behavior. Because many women go topless at the Festival, scars from whipping and other practices were highly visible. In addition, some women campers were disturbed by screams and other sounds coming from neighboring tents.

Lynn avoided the scene and the debates that took place among the crew and organizers over the issue, but she acknowledged that it was a "big deal." Ann observed that some women were saying, "This is a part of my identity. It's important to me, and I want to feel safe in bringing it here," while others were claiming that they didn't feel safe about having these activities occur in Festival space.

In what I would describe as an admirable engagement in building coalition and accommodating difference, it was decided by group consensus that a special S&M–friendly camping area should be created. It was named the Twilight Zone, meaning that there were no rules or restrictions on behavior.

The festival organizers and members seem adept at addressing the issues that emerge within women-only space, and seem genuinely tolerant of diverse views. Ideally, contemporary feminism would be characterized by the same values and practices. The boundaries of women-only space, however, have turned into a contentious issue. In 1993 and 1994, a transsexual camp was formed outside the main camp by individuals who did not fit the "women-identified, women-born-women" attendance criteria of the festival. Writers Riki Ann Wilchins and Leslie Feinberg were among the organizers. Riki Ann Wilchins describes the protest in her/his book *Read My Lips*. The transcamp members felt excluded from the Festival and felt they had the right to attend. They were female-identified men, male-identified women, and others. They felt they had the right to determine their own place in the world of gender, and in fact this claim is one of the strongest and most central assertions of the organized transgender rights movement. It must be remembered that it is only in the 1990s that most regional and college lesbian, gay, bisexual organizations have added transgender to their titles. Transgender activists have struggled to be recognized as part of a queer political coalition and in so doing have gained a great deal of recognition and acceptance.

The boundaries of female space are distinct, however, from the presently accepted boundaries of queer space. The transgender group read their exclusion from the Festival as an infringement of their right to define their genders. The Festival provided a highly visible forum for members of the transgender group to express their feelings about the discrimination they face in mainstream society and to share their experiences of physical and emotional violence. They noted that they came to the Festival for a respite from intolerance and ridicule, from the struggle for the right to exist.

Lynn recalls that the first year transgendered people attended the Festival the demonstration was small, but by the second year it was a well-organized protest. Ann recalls that a similar controversy preceded the inclusion of transgendered individuals in the

San Francisco gay pride parade. At the Michigan Festival the transgendered camp remained officially excluded from the Festival community, but it was recognized and supported by many individuals attending.

Since my discussion with Lynn there have been new developments, and the trans presence at the Festival has become a highly contested issue. Lisa Vogel, speaking for the festival's organizers, reported the following in a public letter to *Lesbian Connection* in 1999:

> On Friday, August 13th, six individuals and a group of supporters from Son of Camp Trans (including several Lesbian Avengers from Chicago and Boston) approached our Box Office and requested tickets to the Festival. They proceeded with the full knowledge of the intent of the Festival to be a womon-born-womon space. In keeping with the Festival's values that no womon's gender ever be questioned on the land, tickets were sold to the six individuals as requested.
>
> The Son of Camp Trans activists then proceeded to the outdoor communal showers in the RV camping area. They took off their clothes and it was apparent to the womyn in and near the showers that two of the Son of Camp Trans activists were anatomically male. The word began to spread that there were men on the land who had shown their penises in the showers. One member of the Son of Camp Trans also stopped by a discussion group for teenage girls at the Community Center, and engaged in an explicit discussion about the clinical aspects of sex change operations. Later, some of the Trans activists began selling Transgender Menace T-shirts outside the main kitchen area (even though sales of products are only permitted in the Crafts Bazaar).[3]

Vogel described the actions the organizers took to deal with the situation. Although the organizers were committed to never questioning any woman's gender, since some attendees of the event would be hurt and insulted by such invasive and unfair interrogation tactics, they met with the group to discuss why they felt that the intrusion was inappropriate. She reports that two members voluntarily agreed to respect the Festival's boundaries and two others agreed not to enter even though they would continue to peacefully demonstrate at the front gate, but organizer Riki Anne Wilchins, who was born male, reentered. Some festivalgoers left early as a sign of protest. Vogel summarized: "We are saddened and angered that political energy is being directed at tearing down womyn's space, instead of at the institutions that still concentrate power and control in patriarchal hands."[4]

This statement applies equally well to attacks on feminist ideology by various factions who are fighting for their right to self-expression within patriarchal culture. The irony is that it is feminism and, in this case, women's space alone that provides the foundation from which such freedom of expression is possible. If anything, the festival, and the contemporary women's movement, bend over backward to make it possible for everyone's needs to be spoken and addressed. What would happen if rebels such as transgender activists entered en masse into a veteran's club, a hockey match, or any other male-dominated space? It is likely they would be physically injured.

In the end, the festival provided an opportune venue for a transgender rights demonstration. Because of it, the legitimate issues they have with patriarchal institutions are brought to the attention of a wide audience of women. Perhaps this exposure lays the basis for a strong political coalition, as has been done within the lesbian, gay, and bisexual community. Its effective organizers are visible and volatile. But, in fact, the allegations they hurl toward the Michigan Womyn's Festival are untrue. According to Vogel, the transgender rights demonstrators were free to enter in and participate in the Festival. Wouldn't their efforts to rebel find a clearer target in a less tolerant setting more broadly representative of American politics? There is a common enemy, after all. The Womyn's Festival is just a little island, as is the women's movement.

I've included these examples to show that the Michigan Womyn's Music Festival, as well as other women's music festivals, can be vibrant sites of interchange and discussion that complicate the picture of contemporary feminist activism. Organizers of and participants at these festivals call for inclusivity and the acceptance of seemingly incongruous positions. They hope to diversify the population of attendees and are making a conscious effort to do so.

The example of the festival, I think, illustrates the position of many feminist/lesbian thinkers who seek to understand and accommodate, rather than judge and exclude, women who do not fit the "type." This is the starting point for women of color who feel uncomfortable allying themselves with white women when other social disparities are conspicuously present. It is also the reason for the growing acceptance of butch/femme sexuality and trans-gendered individuals, as well as S&M practitioners and sex workers who claim to embody a sex-positive culture that defies puritanical restraints on women's sexual expression.

Outside the haven of the Michigan Womyn's Festival, the repressive values of the dominant society are in ample supply. Regardless of the progress feminism has brought, there is little tolerance of alternative gender identities, or rebellious feminist attitudes. The subculture of contemporary feminist and queer rights activists and supporters exists in a safety net that often seems tenuously held together. The daunting reality of the obstacles we face should compel us to cooperate. Even when we as individuals within these communities feel that we have made great progress in overcoming boundaries caused by various types of prejudice, we should remember that not everyone is on our bandwagon and there is still a lot of work to do. We need to form coalitions if for no other reason than that we can't afford not to support each other.

With regard to feminism, the battle is obviously far from over. Dominant society still rewards women who play the wilting flower because such behavior allows entrenched gender categories to remain fixed and knowable, as do flag-waving and public prayer. In 1998, the *New York Times* published an article eroticizing the unlikely pairing of Gloria Steinem and Hugh Hefner as they received awards recognizing their achievements as magazine editors. Although Steinem, who was predictably portrayed as the impossibly intimidating, angry, even castrating feminist, stated, "Remember, it's the right wing that is anti-sex—not feminists," she was positioned throughout the article as the one who destroyed the apparently inevitable sexual energy that could have arched across the room between the two. Hefner, poor old nice guy that he is, was presented as attempting to be charming, flattering, and mildly flirtatious in a gracious sort of way, while Steinem, outraged at being set up by the media, dismissed his charming attempts at appeasement. Meanwhile, his companion, Ms. Rakowitz, tears of sympathy streaking her mascara, stood by her man. "She was so mean to him," she stated afterwards. "She doesn't understand, he's such a nice guy. He's so nice to the women who work for him."[5]

Diatribes against the angry feminist are in amply evident in many venues, but are particularly upsetting coming from the mouths of women. A 1998 issue of *Ms. Magazine* contains a quote by actor Kirstie Alley lifted from *US* magazine. She says, "My definition of feminist is a woman who should have been born in a man's body. Radical chicks with dicks....I don't want to be a girl with a dick. I want to be a girl with a dick in me."[6] Like Ms. Rakowitz, she positions herself as happy to be a woman, which she equates with accepting the power relations between the genders in our present oppressive environment.

This stance has the same roots as attacks on affirmative action in college admissions in California and the de facto resegregation of Boston public schools. The philosophical origin of these two positions is the idea that the individual is responsible for fitting in and that suffering and unhappiness are the penalties paid by individuals who refuse to have a positive and productive outlook, regardless of their situation.

In a sense, Kirstie Alley has a point. Her femininity would be stripped from her if she were an angry feminist, since her sense of femininity depends on male approval, whereas Gloria Steinem's femininity is called into question because she has failed to accept the "gracious" appreciation accorded to her for her physical beauty. Unlike the transgender rights activists at the Michigan Womyn's Music Festival, she has the option of fitting in. A place is accorded her in the echelon of power delineated by dominant society as long as she accepts second place and its rewards without talking back. The wide-ranging feminist community can serve as a pool within which the issues faced by transgendered individuals, gay and lesbian individuals, and individuals who face discrimination on the basis of race and class can find support and opportunities to raise awareness, and yet the dilemma remains that for some women, none of the issues seem to reach home. This may indeed be a source of divisiveness within the feminist community, for if all women are presumed to be somehow linked to feminism through biology, then the indifference of some women may be read as a sign that feminism itself is indifferent to injustice. In a sense, the face of feminism has a tendency to become homogenized and mainstreamed merely by the fact that 50 percent of the population is presumed to lay claim to feminist territory. It is as if a view coming from any woman must be presumed to be feminist because feminism exists in conjunction with the domain of womanhood, when in fact the radicalism of feminism needs to be reasserted again and again for it to exist as a social movement rather than a mildly dissenting outlook that fits comfortably within the status quo. In this sense, it is appropriate that the definitions and boundaries of the Michigan Womyn's Music Festival are challenged, and that these challenges shake up the community and are addressed. Otherwise, nothing changes and evolves.

Is Kirstie Alley's deference to men a way of claiming the privilege available to her as a white woman, limited though it might be? Or is she simply afraid of being perceived as masculine? In her brief testimony she makes it clear that anger, assertion, and defiance are male prerogatives and that any challenge to a narrowly defined female role is ugly and unnatural, not to mention unladylike. And yet she seems unconcerned with the question of the forces of oppression that shaped the code by which she lives. Historical precedents that allowed for the abuse of women (and nonwhites) by assigning them inferior status in a colonial hierarchy are beyond her scope of thinking. Is she banking on the belief that privilege bestowed through race in a racist society will be privilege enough? Or, to put it in other words, does feminism seem redundant to her in light of the fact that she does not see herself as suffering from deprivation, at least in part because of her wealth and race? Perhaps she is also presenting a view of herself as sensual and desirable—putting forth what she thinks the guys want to hear. She wants to be loved and valued, cherished and cared for, to be unquestionably a woman, and feminists such as Gloria Steinem complicate the arena of sensual mores exponentially.

In contrast to Kirstie Alley's renunciation of feminism, Cybill Shepard reflects on her past as a supermodel and the control she lost over the manipulation of her body by advertisers:

> I want to tell the truth, because I was an instrument of that oppression; my career was based on it. I am fortunate that I had that break, but I do feel guilt about it.... I showed the way they would skinny me down when they put me up on a billboard. I think it's mostly about taking up space. And things that make us heavier, rounder, or different shapes are things that are womanly. Men have no problem taking up space. You know, we've gotta be small. We've gotta make ourselves less. Why?[7]

This seems to be a more honest and critical view of her own past decisions and the circumstances that led to them. She raises classic feminist questions and certainly takes a stand of resistance while acknowledging that she has worked within a sexist structure and made her own compromises and relative peace with the situation. However, many of the contemporary artists/writers I include in this paper go a step further to express an even more rebellious attitude of staunch individualism by demanding overarching political upheaval to change dominant power paradigms. For those who challenge feminine gender mandates, freedom of personal expression and defiance of social mandates are closely linked. This form of confrontation, however, is often isolated to the personal arena. It is as if attitude is the sole focus of feminism, rather than movement. Personal freedom, unrestrained and under no authority, is the goal. Community organizing or entering the arena of politics is not even an option, it seems, and certainly not as immediately gratifying as being a rebel who doesn't give a damn about the people in positions of authority and economic and political control.

In addressing the premise of free gender expression as a political act, cultural and gender theorist Susan Bordo delivers the following challenge:

> Perhaps another point of confusion about my position has been that for me—although apparently not for other theorists—questions of "autonomy" and "resistance" are separate ones. That is, whether our actions can be said to be autonomous or "free" is distinct from the question of which of those actions can be said to "resist" a social norm. Questions concerning free will, determinism, and autonomy are either metaphysical questions I couldn't begin to imagine *how* to answer or they are so dependent on definition that they can be answered in any number of equally arbitrary ways.[8]

The desire for personal autonomy, then, can be so enfolded in self-absorption that there is no broader social awareness or intent involved. It is a desire for unhindered freedom and hedonistic self-indulgence, all of which skirts dangerously close to the unarticulated philosophy lurking behind a vast number of commercial images of the person who can do everything and have everything, the wealthy, young, beautiful, and narcissistic young gods who don't have to answer to anybody and don't have to give a damn about anyone. The freedom to be self-indulgent is not necessarily transformative at all. It is, in fact, more of the same old thing.

And yet, for those who have been denied voices, self-sufficiency, freedom, recognized subjective presence, and autonomy, self-indulgence is an act of defiant presence. Whether it is a woman on a commercial treating herself to a chocolate or a hip-hop star moving into a fabulously wealthy, predominantly white neighborhood, images have power and impact, which in our hypermedia age have immediate effects on the perceptions of a broad spectrum of people. If we indeed live in a world of fantasy, as postmodern theorist Jean Baudrillard suggests, where the image has greater impact on consciousness than the actual object referred to, where image-laden icons can attain super-real dimensions and live, like John Kennedy, Jr., beyond his seemingly unreal and unimaginable death, self-creation seems more significant at times than merely buying into the impersonal reality of laws, Congress, and a distant political entity that imposes itself on a given individual's life. Granted, this outlook is not always pragmatic. Even when one considers rushing traffic on a boulevard an extraneous fact of no immediate relevance to oneself, the danger of being run down still exists. Similarly, legislation that dismantles public assistance for women and children, or attacks on affirmative action, gay rights, and so on all have a devastating impact on particular segments of society and should be considered feminist issues that cannot be ignored. Still, personal empowerment through fantasy and self-creation can be a consciously defiant act of self-determination and can have wide-ranging effects on the individual and extended community. The issue that is often overshadowed, however, is that one's choices, in and of themselves, are not necessarily aimed at transformation or enacted with a deep understanding of broader significance. Sometimes narcissism is just narcissism.

Diane DiMassa's comic-book character Hothead Paisan offers an example of transformation through defiant autonomy. Although her actions seem unconstructive and chaotic at first glance, Hothead challenges her oppressors with attitude, appearance, and defiance. Hothead Paisan is an unapologetically violent lesbian feminist who feels at home blowing away white male heterosexist figures who blather inanities and rely on brute force and unquestioning self-assurance of male privilege to make their points. They are typically drawn as monstrous, utterly stupid, unconscious beings. In one strip, Hothead is taunted on the highway by two men in a car on her way to Provincetown, Massachusetts, a well-known summer hot spot for queer people. Claiming that she "specializes in blow-u-away jobs," she pulls out a gun and announces "I'm not your fuckin' spritz-head girlfriend, I'm Hothead Paisan." In neat comic-book fashion, she demolishes men and car, leaving no trace, while women passengers in other cars applaud.[9]

The existence of such a character points to what I can only call an alternate universe in which Hothead is unstoppable. Her character, exaggerated for effect, is the embodiment of a defiant woman. She's not just angry, she's pissed, and she gets even. Her hair is spiked. She wears leather and drinks coffee to the point of intoxication. She's selfish and enraged. She's unpleasant and impolite. She's lesbian—and definitely a man-hater—and she makes no bones about it. Her image defies sexist patterns of judgment against women, defies heterosexist imperatives, and defies the gentler, kinder images of necessarily egalitarian, usually vegetarian, lesbian feminists of earthy goddess lineage. She is not merely creating an ideal separate world for herself, she is creating a world whose very existence busts apart, literally, the dominant storyline of the sexist world she encounters on a panel-by-panel basis. There is nothing innocuous about Hothead Paisan.

And yet her anger is more a state of mind, a fashion almost, rather than a means of transformation. Her end goal is only to exist as a rebel, spraying her disruptive chaos like spit in all directions around her. Her aim is to affirm her existence as a defiant being, as she is necessarily read by the dominant heterosexist patriarchal world in which she lives. Her existence has been branded as defiance, and since she cannot escape that position, she stomps and revels in it and becomes a perpetual warrior. She exaggerates and enjoys the freakish evilness read into her and turns it full force on her attackers. While possibly creating a sense of a limited territory in which she is free among other "queer" outcasts, she is not intent on addressing or interacting with the patriarchal society that has banished her. It's all-out war against everyone and everything. It's a state of being.

In another set of panels, her resentment is aimed specifically at "politically correct" constructions of lesbian identity. In response to unseen tormentors, Hothead rants:

> Listen, some rigid dyke with a pole up her ass once told me I wasn't a radical lesbian *in her book* cause I eat meat and talk about sex out loud!! She was trying to lay all the conditions on me, and then she's out there protesting + lobbying for rights an' acceptance! What a fuckin' *hypocrite*!! ...

She adds, a few panels later:

> I get as much shit from the politically correct police as I do from anybody else!! What could be worse than being in the closet around gay people?[10]

Her desire for autonomy is a wish for everyone to get off her back, including other lesbians who don't share her views. In her rampant individualism, she eschews the possibility of community activism, except for the coming together of a group of women like herself to bust things apart. Transformation of society on a grand scale becomes a moot point. Like a heroin addict, she's already attained her freedom. Her anger is her badge and her identity. She is a woman only for herself, and she is uninterested in a public reading of her identity. In this sense, she is the antithesis of feminine assimilationist Kirstie Alley. There is nowhere left for Hothead to get to. She's an end in herself. She has constructed herself as the antithesis of who she refuses to be.

According to Susan Bordo's description of autonomy and resistance, Hothead, although aiming for autonomy, is embedded in resistance to cultural norms. Moreover, Hothead is a fantasy figure, and as such, actually "acts" in her world. She is a self-absorbed dreamer who imagines her freedom into existence by ignoring the resistance she meets; her resistance is only theoretical. This may be enough to live on if nothing else is available, but it is not, in a strict sense, transformative of society as a whole, since there is no momentum to carry us beyond the present to create a new and better social system. This form of resistance and defiance rests on the notion that individual freedom and autonomy, uninfluenced by social mores, are possible. Yet, ironically, it is exactly this oversight that shackles the rebel to the very images and issues being resisted.

Susan Bordo asks:

> Am I behaving autonomously when I choose my clothes? If I imagine autonomy as having to do with interpretation and creative interaction with cultural forms, I would say I have "autonomy" in choosing my clothes. But if this is my definition of autonomy, then it applies just as

> well to just about every conceivable human activity beyond the purely instinctual, including many of those performed in conditions of outright servitude. If, however, I define "autonomy" as requiring that I act without the mediation of culture, then no, I certainly do not have "autonomy" in picking my clothes. But what actions *would* qualify as autonomous in this way? However I define autonomy, the cultural world is impinging on me in the same concrete ways.[11]

Contemporary feminism is a movement that acknowledges that things are always more complex than theory can portray. Its proponents recognize the contradictions that arise when we try to force individual lives to match idealized political stances.

In Leslie Heywood's *Third Wave Agenda,* four Berkeley grad students talk about their own perceptions of themselves as women. Anna Cox describes her transition to butch-style fashion choices after being sexually harassed by a male professor:

> And that was when I pierced my nose and cut my hair and stopped wearing dresses. Essentially, I said to myself, "oh, this is what's gonna happen if I play the 'femme' role. Men will feel free to do this to me." ...this man was slimy—I didn't like him, you know, and it really freaked me out that he felt free to do that. And I do think it was because of the way I dressed.[12]

Anna Cox, Annalee Newitz, Jillian Sandell, and Freya Johnson all note that when they dress for power in the professional world, such as when they teach, they wear pants and do the masculine thing. It gives them a sense of agency. Later in the piece, Annalee Newitz states that her basic justification for being male-identified, as a woman, is that, "transgressiveness is good, subversiveness is good."[13]

These women clearly see themselves as nonconformists and as people who freely experiment with gender representation. They acknowledge the connection between gender representation and power in a male-dominated society. In their articulations, being masculine is about having power. Being feminine is about being sensual, vulnerable, daring, alive, and erotic, and they want it all. Their article presents a complex picture of gender.

Defiance can also take the form of women embracing and defining their own sensuality. I attended a performance one evening by the group Utopia Rising, described in their brochure as avant-garde lesbian performance artists. The "permission slip" to attend (passed out before the show) included a vow to "overthrow the patriarchy and take a women's studies class."

The performance by Jess Dobkin, Erica Cho, and Jayne Weber included an emcee in a skin-tight tiger suit with bulging dildo; a woman hammering, eating, and spitting up marshmallows; a puppet dance with strings tied to the breasts of one of the women; and popcorn for the audience in bags that read "hot and salty." It was a relief to be freed even momentarily of the haunting vestiges of Sunday school and my Presbyterian upbringing. After their performance I felt like the world was an open book of possibilities once again, and being a woman no longer felt like a handicap or disadvantage.

For sex-positive lesbian/feminists, both public and privately internalized restrictions on female sexual expression are results of patriarchal control. The creation of a new context, of a "utopia rising," provides a ground for assertion of self-will and presence through sexual reconfigurations of power dynamics, even of gender itself. It is more than the freedom to shout. It is the freedom to invite the stares; to wear tattoos, body piercings, leather, and even lipstick; to feel sexy and to own that sexuality. It is, more than anything, an escape from the numbing self-denial of the sexless, desireless, absolutely controlled configuration of womanhood.

As I read through more comic books I came upon another image that illustrates the complexity of gender issues contemporary lesbian feminists face. In an Alison Bechdel collection, Mo reflects on the good old days when she knew that "monogamy and romantic love were just male supremacist constructs designed to keep women in their place." She applauds herself for having become a lesbian who strives "to transcend outmoded paradigms of behavior" but later admits that "the picket fence would be awfully nice."[14] Many of us face these questions and contradictions about what we are actually looking for as feminists when the old patterns of masculine-feminine relationships have been blown apart. We may try to reconstruct a past based on the lure of security and the image of being settled in the American dream, but once we become aware of the political reality of those images we cannot easily go back to patterns of subjugation.

Sex-positive dyke art and literature, however, are not necessarily liberating. Ground-breaking confrontational and shocking statements, in and of themselves, do not imply a progressive political intent. Confrontational sexual images are sometimes used as a safety net or a kind of insulation from criticism. I also feel cautious about a political agenda based on the premise of self-gratification. In one sense, this is because white male–centered self-gratification is the norm in our patriarchal media culture. All other human beings are seen as disposable and are posited as existing for male pleasure. Simply turning this paradigm on itself by exploiting others or reversing patterns of domination is not necessarily a liberatory act. However, representations of such alternatives in film, liberating, or art do have the power to stir things up, and for this reason alone they may be included by some as part of feminist discourse.

As a filmmaker, Monica Treut has dealt with issues involving S&M sex, butch/femme roles, transgendered people, and sex-positive culture. Her portrayals of lesbians are varied, and her characters are not always nice or conventionally moral. And they are definitely sexual. In *My Father Is Coming*, a young German woman in New York is trying to make a career as an actress. She goes to an audition that turns out to be for the role of a sex worker, a woman who makes erotic films. The woman tries to join in the energy of it, but after a few minutes she says it's not for her and leaves. In the hall she meets a handsome man, tall, dark-haired, and oddly intense. In a bumbling, direct sort of way he asks her out and then offers to drive her to work.

Once in the car, he stares and stares at himself in the rearview mirror. When she asks why, he says "to remember who I am." We later learn that he is a female to male transsexual. Until that moment, however, I was lulled into the conventionality of the script. The tension I felt as a viewer was my concern that she was getting into a car with a man she didn't even know; a man who was acting oddly. Sure, he was handsome and nice, but he still posed a threat in my mind. Once his gender was revealed, that sense shifted. I wanted the limits pushed. I wanted them to kiss; fear was replaced by excitement about the unknown.

Treut has stated that "straight people can see the film and enjoy a lesbian, a gay man, a transsexual person. I don't like to make all these divisions between people; I'd like to go beyond that."[15] In this sense, her work defies stereotypes because she shakes up the fixed ideas of gender and sexual morality held by her characters and imagined viewers alike.

In Monica Treut's film *Seduction, the Cruel Woman*, she seems to be playing with the idea that submitting to art, like submitting to sexual S&M play, is a consensual act. In this film, a male journalist in a conservative suit interviews a dominatrix who engages in sexual acts with her underlings, who act as obedient servants and allow themselves to be humiliated by her. They are men and women, and they find a compulsive sense of gratification in trying to please a woman who is very difficult to please. The interviewer sees himself as a neutral figure, but she immediately dispenses with that notion. His gaze and his curiosity, like those of the movie viewer, make him a participant. If he wants to know more, he has to submit, and he does want to know more. He is humiliated in various ways, and perhaps because he is a man, this film somehow disrupts the dominant male-centered paradigm. It certainly caused protests in Germany when it opened, although it also did at a woman's film screening in San Francisco.[16] It is a confrontational film, but the images in it are not liberatory, nor, I think, are they meant to be, except for the fact that they unearth hidden and unexplained impulses. The act of confrontation itself, however, is meant to be a political act of expanding borders of perception and acceptance.

There is a darkness to the film, an uncomfortable edge tinged with the knowledge that one could just as easily be watching the filming of a torture scene or rape, and I was left to ask what the difference was. The acts were consensual, yes, but I think the film did a great job of showing that we are not always in charge of our consent or of our fantasies. We often leave the space of their source in a deliberate mire because erotic gratification is about giving over rather than analyzing. The film itself is full of dimly lit gray-walled scenes. It takes place in a grim city setting. My memory of the film is not of daylight or green trees but of dim recesses. In fact, for me, the most striking scene in the film takes place in a grungy alley at night, where two people begin making love surrounded by filth and dirt and nothing redeeming in sight. The setting is gray and valueless, urban and bleak, suggesting a sense of the violence and worthlessness that the indifference of modern industrial society engenders. It serves as an indictment of the brutality of the social structure that confines and brutalizes the individual. Even so, I felt degraded as I watched this film. I felt a sense of hopelessness overcome me, a sense of an absence of love in human relations, and in that absence the presence of the lowest form of human interaction—dominance, exploitation, and self-gratification.

bell hooks argues that:

> certain feminist writings by lesbian women on S/M discuss what role-playing is in terms of power. A woman can take on ritualized role-playing in terms of confronting the dragon, and realize that in the confrontation of that dragon (through role-playing), it no longer has power over you.[17]

And yet, even here there is an assumption, one I share, though I don't know quite why, that being lesbian-centered creates another context. What would be sleazy and grotesque in a heterosexual context, say, is given sanction in a feminist context because it wrests control of the erotic away from male-centered gratification and focuses inevitably on the female body/subject, whether as dominant or submissive participant. And yet, as an individual, I choose not to be uncritical of my own actions, or even of my desires, and I'm not sure it makes sense to suspend judgment across the board for any cause.

In an interview entitled "Sadomasochism: Not About Condemnation," Audre Lorde states:

> Sadomasochism in the lesbian-feminist community cannot be seen as separate from the larger economic and social issues surrounding our communities. It is reflective of a whole social and economic trend in this country.... Sadomasochism is congruent with other developments going on in this country that have to do with dominance and submission, with disparate power—politically, culturally, and economically.[18]

This analysis ties in quite well with Monica Treut's movie because there is a social context to veiled desires for revenge and defiant death and for giving in to end the struggle. But does S&M sex disrupt power hierarchies? Why do people feel it does? Maybe it allows some individuals to "feel like women" and still be defiant feminists.

Two years ago, I attended a showing of a video made by some friends for a competition at a local gay bar. I happened to be sitting next to a friend of mine who is African American and her friend, named Diane, who is also African American. Four films were shown, three by gay men. As one of the films started rolling, my mind was wandering, waiting for the lesbian film to come on. Suddenly Diane exclaimed, "That film just said 'Kunta Kinte.' What's going on? Did you hear that?"

"I wasn't listening," I answered. The next scene that emerged on the screen was that of an African-American man on his knees weeding a garden. He wore a collar and leash held by a white man, who was advertising a new brand of weed killer called Kunta Kinte.

While I admit I sat dumbly looking on, not knowing what to do, Diane stood up and began yelling loudly, "I can't believe this! This is racist! This is fucking racist!" The film stopped, and the owner of the bar ran after her as she left through the door. Diane refused to return, but the rest of the group present, mostly white women, agreed to stay and discuss the film. The men who made the film claimed it was a joke, a kind of S&M parody, just as S&M itself is parody or role-playing. They felt that it wasn't "real" racism because the actors were best friends and their intention had only been to make a funny skit. And yet the S&M symbolism of subordination treated as tantalizing was disturbingly mixed with racial domination, also meant, I assume, on some unfathomable level, to be sexy. I find the notion abhorent. But if the basic idea behind the sexiness of S&M sex is its outrageousness, its trangression of taboos and boundaries regarding human relations, then it is apparent that transgression can become an end in itself. The film clip may have been a release of pent-up impulses created by a cultural storyline learned in childhood, but this example certainly could not be held up as one with the potential to transform our society into a more free and egalitarian form.

The desire for the freedom to express whatever one wants is an infantile urge, unmediated by rationality and moral purpose. The horrible racist image presented in the film clip was a perfect example of the need I feel to be constantly vigilant in our critical thinking when we assert the right to feel and express "whatever comes up." If racist images emerge in dominant-submissive scenarios, or if sexist images arise, it is too easy to claim that it is an accidental association of circumstance. Domination, whether on the scale of national imperialism, society's prevalent sexist attitudes, or the personal interactions of two individuals, must be questioned and scrutinized. Watching the short clip that night, I had a similar painful feeling to what I felt watching Treut's *Seduction*, that it went too far, and I was unwittingly agreeing to participate in something with which I was wholly uncomfortable.

I was horrified by the occurrence in the bar, but in reflecting back on what happened I realize that it was Diane's courageous act to challenge what was happening that focused all of our attention on it. Part of me had just wanted to skip over it as something unpleasant and get on with the evening. But Diane's reaction made me take in what had happened and the significance of it. In the same way, I feel that an acceptance of confrontation and alternative sexualities as liberatory by the feminist community is an attempt to assume a stance of neutrality when in fact there is none. Being neutral means going with the flow, in this case the flow of racism or inhumane violence. And yet many contemporary feminists seem to be taking a "neutral" live-and-let-live stance towards S&M in the interest of embracing personal freedom. In looking at the Michigan Womyn's Music Festival as an analogy for the contemporary feminist community, I hoped to show the importance of inclusiveness and acceptance, and yet, in the case of S&M, uncritical acceptance also seems to be a philosophically troublesome position.

I can't help agreeing with Audre Lorde that critical thinking has been responsible for a great deal of the progress toward human dignity in the past decades, and though I refuse to censure others, I also refuse to simply sit back and say live and let live. This holds true whether we're speaking of a Ku Klux Klan rally or of art imbued with racist or sexist images, or with other images that degrade human dignity.

We must always be willing to ask the question, therefore, if affirming difference and individuality should always encompass tolerance for every viewpoint or artistic expression. This is the question many people would prefer to leave alone because there's no simple answer, but we must answer it. Absolute tolerance is as corrupting a force as absolute intolerance, yet we live in a society that represses sexuality, particularly in women, since codes of chaste behavior apply almost exclusively to women. This oppressive force not only seeks to numb and sterilize female existence, it also seeks to control women. If we as women seek autonomy and a sense of political selfhood, we cannot overlook the need we feel to own our bodies. For too long many of us have tried to deny, or even erase, our bodies. (In Cybill Shepherd's case, her body was literally erased in her modeling shots.) I think we as women need to explore the power we have as sensual beings, because in sensuality we remake, redefine, and revisualize ourselves, and this act, in and of itself, is powerful. However, we also need to be conscious of how we redefine ourselves with this power and to continually ask ourselves if this is where we want to be and why we've made the choices we have.

In the end, there seem to be a great many reasons to celebrate rebellion and revolutionary confrontations in the sphere of individual expression. However, the purpose of, and the audience for, such confrontations often seem random and not directed toward obvious political transformation. Whether we're theorists, activists, or rebels, we should think about who and what we're rebelling against. As the Michigan Womyn's Music Festival illustrates, the women's movement has created the ground from which gay, lesbian, transgender, and racial representation and a myriad of other issues can be discussed. The movement is broad enough to transform itself each time a new voice or a new view is raised because its goal is to create the possibility for women to discover what it means to live in freedom. Confrontational images that jar us from our ordinary views may well be part of this transformation and part of the future vision of feminism. They certainly serve a revolutionary purpose, and yet we must be critical observers of this flood of new creations. We must ask which of the views presented we actually endorse and which ones lure us with the promise that breaking the rules will bring us freedom and pleasure while in fact they lead us to places we would prefer not to go.

CHAPTER 4

Resistance and Liberation

For within living structures defined by profit, by linear power, by institutional dehumanization, our feelings were not meant to survive. Kept around as unavoidable adjuncts or pleasant pastimes, feelings were expected to kneel to thought as women were expected to kneel to men. But women have survived. As poets.

—Audre Lorde[1]

The only two things I've ever loved in my life are dancing and writing. I have a belief that if you don't love something, you'll never be great at it.

—Maya Angelou[2]

As a student and theorist I have sometimes felt trapped in claustrophobic confinement in the field of women's studies and by the label "feminist," a fact I admit with a certain amount of trepidation, since it is, after all, my primary area of study. But the issue of women's rights at times seems to be corralled off from other human rights concerns, and as a result my interests as a theorist are assumed by many to be exclusively female. Such is not the case. I view women's oppression as intricately linked to other forms of oppression, such as racism, homophobia, and classism. This being the case, I have decided to experiment in this chapter by breaking down all boundaries and categories of classification and focusing instead on the process of oppression itself with the specific aim of defining the pathways individuals have used to counter and sometimes overcome the dehumanizing forces that inflict on them unfair and unsupported labels, judgments, laws, and acts of violence.

The scope of my project seems to have become something more than I imagined it would. I thought at first that I was examining the different conceptions of feminism that live side by side in our contemporary society as reflected in culture and fiction. As time went by I became aware that I was also addressing the apathy and nihilism feminists of our time face with the knowledge that the bold political movements of the 1960s and 1970s have not eliminated oppression against women, who turn instead to dramatic acts of art or self-expression to prove that they can exist in defiance of the forces working against them in their quest for freedom and self-determination. The laying out of personal ground, the claim of the right to exist even in the midst of an oppressive social environment, is a process I call "defiant feminism." When one applies this concept to other forms of oppression, the idea becomes "defiant humanism." My interest is in the survival of the individual, and my study is of the processes through which the individual survives. Again and again the authors I continue to read, while documenting previously silenced discrimination, nonetheless offer a message of hope and survival, seemingly against all odds.

Because my focus is on survival, this essay is the first in this collection to include several male authors. Have I crossed the boundaries of feminist theory? Yes, for two reasons. First, I would like to be able to address feminism within a greater context of oppression, especially since many of the authors I have addressed so far have done exactly this in their works of fiction. I feel that it is possible to shift perspectives and allow the female-centeredness of feminism to recede into the background without disappearing. This is an experiment. It is not meant to negate the legitimacy of focusing specifically on women's issues, which I do elsewhere in this treatise. Second, the question always arises for me of who and what exactly the enemy is. When I speak of oppressive forces, I am aware that I am circumventing the fact that individuals who hold violent views and act to humiliate and annihilate others are not merely "forces." They are human beings making choices, often because of circumstances and sometimes because of the belief that they are acting in self-preservation. I don't mean to let anyone off the hook, and yet categories used to designate these individuals are in many cases merely reductive and inaccurate stereotypes. After all, some of the best feminists I know are men… really!

When I use a kind of literary shorthand to get to my main point without pausing to explain myself deeply, phrases such as patriarchy, white male privilege, the privilege of masculine subjectivity, and so on emerge, and I always feel a great deal of discomfort in using such inadequate language. In fact, shortcuts such as these fuel the claims of anti-feminists that we are "feminazis," "man-haters" and other crude designations. To be labeled and dismissed as pathological critics of the male gender defeats the purpose of reinventing and organizing our culture. Furthermore, such language implies that masculine behavior is innately ingrained and unchanging rather than socially constructed by culturally situated masculine ideals. It is important to define very clearly who the enemy is. The enemy is a culturally embedded frame of mind, a force of history, transposed onto the individual. The enemy is also that frame of mind held by an individual who is not willing to look beyond his/her own circumstances and needs or show concern for the welfare of other human beings. It is a frame of mind so focused on individuality that the commonality of humanity, indeed, of all living beings in the natural world, is overlooked. Obviously, a society that values an elite privileged segment of individuals over others contributes to creating a selfish and destructive class of oppressors.

Those who were not meant to survive under the suppression of colonizers…have survived. The very title of Audre Lorde's *Sister Outsider* speaks to the fact that there is a way to survive, even when the dominant message is that one is not meant to be happy and fulfilled because such are the pleasures of a privileged few. Historical precedents such as the enslavement of African Americans—which included bondage, imprisonment, forced labor, rape, torture, and death—created a reality in which survival itself seems miraculous. For Native Americans, likewise, American expansion is not cause for celebration but rather a nagging disease that will not subside. The cultural memories of slaughter, starvation, imprisonment, rape, torture, forced labor, death, and life in forced submission rest like ropes around the necks of contemporary human beings whose cultural memory banks also include memories of the gentleness and intelligence of the victims of such horrific oppression. Pain has become for many people an unwelcome but insistent aspect of cultural identity, and the past cannot be ignored if the injustices of today are ever to be understood and addressed. Those who do not have the full cultural memories of our national past see the poverty, lack of education, unstable home life, alcoholism, and drug use of the survivors of racial oppression as inevitable, as if the atrocities of the past have no consequences in the present.

Women, likewise, have historically been excluded from the right to exist with human dignity and respect, a right that should be all-inclusive but has instead become the privilege of a select group that poses as neutral and inclusive. Respect should not be a privilege. Human dignity should be a neutral ideal that applies to everyone, but that is not the case. The very utterance of the term survival implies hardship and destitution, exploitation and misery.

The term survival is often used in the context of physical survival. But Audre Lorde speaks of an equally important kind of survival, a kind of survival that is essential to culture—the survival of poets. The focus of my study is this other sort of survival, the survival of spirit, the indescribable and profound source of hope and human dignity. Survival can rise out of the depths of despair to become a mysterious force in itself, even when oppressors proclaim that it is impossible. Defiance, tenacity, and the willingness to be vitally present, even when threatened with erasure, are qualities that speak to the existence of a power within the human psyche that is able to create, or perhaps affirm, a personal reality that cannot be reduced to flat physicality and that resists annihilation even in the face of deadening, wide-scale oppression.

But those who would dominate and subjugate others insist on a narrow definition of reality that places them on top of the heap. To be upheld, a political system based on the suppression of human rights requires the denial of individual viewpoints and the denial of the existence of inner life and the right to occupy a domain of personal consciousness. In this light, the spiritual force I am speaking of is the presence of individual consciousness that questions absolute reality, absolute truth, and natural order. Claims to absolute truth are based on the hidden premise that only one reading of reality can exist at a time and that truth is manufactured by those with the greatest power. Such truth is extremely narrow in scope and requires a rendering of reality that excludes individual perception, experience, or dreams in favor of a physical rendering of obvious, observable evidence to be taken at face value as a lasting, sanctioned vision of the way things have always been and always will be. But even if the body is imprisoned, cannot a person dream? With great effort, with great luck and tenacity, it seems so, and the significance of dreams, aspirations, fantasies, and faith should never be underestimated.

The project of survival through defiance and tenacity, tempered in some cases by practical compliance, is transformative and earth-shattering in its scope. Poets who look at death and suffering defy oppressors who believe there is no witness to the atrocities they commit. Poets elevate humanity with their compassion in the face of unimaginable horrors. One such poet is Carolyn Forché, who writes of her experiences in El Salvador in the 1980s in a collection entitled *The Country Between Us*. In the poem "Return" she speaks of the victims who suffer the aftermath of politically motivated torture:

> They cup their own parts
> with their bedsheets and move themselves
> slowly, imagining bracelets affixing
> their wrists to a wall where the naked
> are pinned, where the naked are tied open
> and left to the hands of those who erase
> what they touch.[3]

Rather than treating the lives of Salvadorian political dissidents and human rights supporters as insignificant and distant, Forche went into the battle and looked with her own eyes at what was happening in El Salvador with the aid and acceptance of the United States. She forcefully extricated herself from the numbing "reality" of her country's worldview, which simply overlooked the human consequences and denied responsibility for the civil war. Forché refuses to comply passively with the complacency of sheltered and well-fed Americans; she writes poetry to express her troubled state of mind. Indifference, she implies, is a key ingredient in the large-scale human atrocities happening worldwide. Of the acts of the torturers, which we surely should have prevented, she states:

> We are all erased
> by them, and no longer resemble decent
> men. We no longer have the hearts,
> the strength, the lives of women.
> Your problem is not your life as it is
> in America, not that your hands, as you
> tell me, are tied to do something. It is
> that you were born to an island of greed
> and grace where you have this sense
> of yourself as apart from others. It is
> not your right to feel powerless. Better
> people than you were powerless.[4]

Here she informs us of that to which we have been oblivious and makes the case that we should all step outside the shared reality of those in power and join with the outsiders—in this case, the oppressed—because that is where humanity lies. Inhumanity and indifference mark the domain of the oppressors, the default zone of residence for many Americans. When Forché returns to the United States, she finds the vivid images she encounters shockingly distant from the other land that is now part of her reality. The turmoil is churning in her observations of "iced drinks and paper umbrellas, clean toilets and Los Angeles palm trees moving like lean women."[5] The contrast of this scenery with where she has come from brings America's insular isolation into focus.

Carolyn Forché is engaged in a struggle with indifference as much as she is engaged in a struggle with military dictators and killers. Her poetry is meant to move "born in the USA" Americans by bringing to the forefront images of inhuman lack of concern for the well-being of others and by showing that all of us who fail to react share in the acts that violence engenders. She is saying that the fact that our world is unspeakably violent is not someone else's problem. As readers we too feel queasy with her in her poem "The Colonel" as she sits down to dinner in the colonel's barricaded estate while American television plays in the background. Everything is eerily familiar and ordinary, almost America-like, perhaps too America-like, and so somehow unreal and displaced. Over this surreal scene the moon swings on a "bare black cord" over a house which carries a displaced echo of America's insulation. Its serenity is hollow. After dinner is finished, the colonel leaves the table and returns. Forché writes that from an ordinary sack:

> He spilled many human ears on the table. They were like dried peach halves. There is no other way to say this. He took one of them in his hands, shook it in our faces, dropped it into a water glass. It came alive there. I am tired of fooling around he said. As for the rights of anyone, tell your people they can go fuck themselves. He swept the ears to the floor with his arm and held the last of his wine in the air. Something for your poetry, no? he said. Some of the ears on the floor caught this scrap in his voice. Some of the ears on the floor were pressed to the ground.[6]

Each of the ears is a ghost who in death shines forth, pulling out of us what shreds of compassion and emotion we can muster. They are a force even in their absence. And the colonel, who is present, is absent in spirit, devoid of the redeeming emotions that might have made him human. He is barely recognizable as a human being. The lives of the dead are now whispers heard by the poet, ears upturned in hope and expectation and turned to the ground in resignation, drawing comfort from the mysterious earth from which they came. The dead are gone, but the poet hears them. There is a witness, and because of her words we too feel the earth reel beneath our feet.

Another writer whose creative arts focus on bitter realities that would otherwise lie silently muted is Bette Bao Lord, who shares stories she collected during visits to China as the wife of a diplomat in *Legacies: A Chinese Mosaic*. They are stories of bare survival in trying circumstances. An author's note before the table of contents states: "The stories I tell are true and because they are I had no choice but to disguise the people who lived them." Many are from political prisoners who have suffered under China's communist regime. And in these stories a vision of the fragility of survival emerges. She opens with the following illustration:

> A dear friend who, as I write, is in a Chinese prison once told me this tale:
>
> For want of something to do, a prisoner gleaned from the sweepings of the shop floor tiny bits of glittering wire, which he deposited in a bottle. Years passed. On the day he was freed, there was nothing to take with him to mark the passage of those years except the bottle, and so he carried it away.
>
> Back home, he rose and he ate and he slept at the exact hours the warden had decreed. Too old to work anymore, he spent his days pacing, the exact space of his long confinement—four paces forward, four paces back, four paces forward, four paces back.

> For want of something to do, one day he smashed the bottle to count how many tiny bits of glittering wire he had collected. He wept. At his feet lay broken glass, and a clump of wires rusted solid in the shape of a bottle.[7]

The person telling the tale would be utterly silenced if Lord were not speaking for him, since he is in prison and might not survive the ordeal physically or otherwise. He is being created in reaction to the cruelty of his oppressors. He describes his suffering as a shutting down of the mind. This image reminds me of a photo of an elderly Tibetan monk named Kalu Rinpoche (who has since died) that was given to me in India. In it, he gazes sadly down at a dove he holds in his hands, his eyes filled with sympathy, his angular face drawn and calm. I later met an American Buddhist nun who described to me the meaning of the photo, since she had been present when it was taken. He had bought the dove in a marketplace in order to set it free. Saving animals is a common Buddhist practice. The dove, however, knew only a life confined to a metal cage. It clung to his hands, cooing in fear, with no intention of leaving.

Of course, the old monk held Tibet in his hands. For years and years grown into decades the refugees in India held dear their dream of return to a free Tibet. They dreamed of raising again thousands of temples long since ravaged into rubble by bombs and greedy traders sifting through the ruins in search of discarded treasure. In the meantime, the waiting changed them all. Back in the ruins of Tibet, their children studied Chinese in school and reported their parents to the communist authorities. Re-education squads in prison and in the street repeated again and again the one and only reality allowed public existence, and with threats, torture, and death silenced those still capable of being moved to public outcry, to feelings of human empathy and dissent against violence. Life had been pressed from life. Like the bird who should have flown, freedom was quelled in Tibet. And what was harbored deep inside, protected and imagined safe through a passing storm, had grown silent and unable to speak.

The extreme example of frozen fear Bette Bao Lord presents is the frame of mind Audre Lorde warns of in the quote at the chapter's start when she speaks of institutions that crush feeling and grind the individual out of existence. Toni Morrison writes of this kind of survival—the kind that is resigned, reduced to bare bones, unable to ask for more—in *Beloved.* Her characters struggle for the meanest existence against a backdrop of hopelessness and countless unredeemable losses. The image of Sethe—based on a historical account—killing her child so that she might "survive," so that she might not be brought down by the misery of living when life has been stripped away, speaks of similar desperation.

According to Howard Zinn, infanticide was a relatively common practice among the Indians of the Caribbean who were enslaved by the Spaniards to work in mines searching for gold following Columbus's arrival. Zinn presents the eyewitness account of Catholic priest Bartolome de las Casas:

> Thus husbands and wives were together only once every eight or ten months and when they met they were so exhausted and depressed on both sides ... they ceased to procreate. As for the newly born, they die early because their mothers, overworked and famished, had no milk to nurse them, and for this reason, while I was in Cuba, 7000 children died in three months. Some mothers even drowned their babies from sheer desperation.[8]

Such a context makes one woman's seemingly inexplicable act seem like a reasonable choice, or at least a choice as reasonable as any. Of American Indians in the continental United States, Zinn reports that only 300,000 were left at the turn of the century, "from the original million or more." By 1860, the United States held four million African Americans in slavery. Deeply entrenched beliefs regarding their own sense of superiority were necessary to allow the perpetrators of these heinous crimes to carry out their madness.[9]

For many contemporary Native American writers, it seems almost as if a story cannot be told without the context of the losses of the past in mind, because for Native Americans, identity itself has come to abide in resistance to the oppressive omnipresence of the dominant white culture. Because of this, a tone of speaking back is almost always present, an intonation again and again of another version of the past and, consequently, another image of the present.

For example, in a short story called "Hitching" by Carlson Vicenti, a young male narrator describes the scenery that unravels during his hitchhiking journey, and his observations are often biting and bitter. In one passage, he states:

> A rancher pulls up in a pick-up truck and gives me a ride. His dog sits up front and I sit in the back. The rancher is probably afraid I'll give the dog fleas. I sit back and think. In the course of two hours, I have seen every red-cheeked, bony, corn-fed, wholesome American caricature painted by Norman Rockwell.[10]

Later, at a circus, he runs for cover from the visions of people on display as freaks because of physical deformities:

> I look up to breathe and a chubby redneck boy points his cotton candy cone at me and says, "Look Mom, an Indian Man. Look Mom, an Indian man. Look mom, an Indian, an Indian, Indian, Indian."[11]

His perspective is one that necessarily speaks back to the comments directed at him. His anger is evident, as is his contempt for the narrow-mindedness and ignorance with which he is viewed as an Indian.

The presence of the past is unavoidable in contemporary Native American writers. The past is invoked and contrasted with the indifference of modern culture, even in the case of a writer with a nonconfrontational, welcoming style of prose, such as Joseph Marshall, III, whose stories take place almost exclusively within a secluded Native American context. In "Cozy By the Fire," he tells the story of a truant officer at a reservation high school caught in a North Dakota snowstorm on a rural road. The premise is simple and seemingly unconfrontational.

> Since most of the local residents were Indians, the county highway maintenance officials were of the opinion that the Bureau of Indian Affairs should maintain the roads in this area, despite the fact that the road had been appropriated by the right of eminent domain by the county years ago. As result of constant tit-for-tat legal brinkmanship, the roads in the Black Pipe District were not paved and always the last to be plowed after heavy snows.[12]

Already a tone is set that provides a context of the neglect suffered by the Native American community. As the storm worsens, his character, Jeremy Blue, faces the prospect of a freezing night in the cab of his stalled truck. Jeremy experiences at close hand the power of the values of his culture to sustain when he follows a glowing light off the side of the road even though his rational mind knows that no one lives there. "To the east the light seemed brighter, a persistent glow, a beckoning hope. He paused momentarily, wondering if he was hallucinating, but concluded that the only unknown was the light. Every other miserable thing—the snow, the piercing cold, the stalled truck—was real enough."[13] The image of threatened survival, of life on the very edge, is cogently present, as is a hope that appears as if from nowhere, which in fact turns out to be a real yet dreamlike connection to ancestors whose presence sustains him.

When Jeremy reaches the house, the door opens, and in a glow of warmth and soft light from kerosene lamps, he is greeted by a "slight, almost frail" old Lakota woman with long gray braids and gentle eyes and her husband, equally old and calm. Their clothing, like the furnishings of the house, are old-fashioned and handmade. The couple, who speak only Lakota, graciously offer him deer stew and skillet bread and later unroll a bedroll on the floor for him. In the morning, overcome with gratitude, Jeremy offers them money, which they refuse. When he returns the next day with groceries, the house is mysteriously gone. He leaves the groceries in a gesture of gratitude.[14]

The story, sweet and heartwarming, speaks of a connectedness between the people of the present and their ancestors, who live on in spirit. Jeremy's immediate survival depended on their generosity, but the story also suggests that the events of the stormy night held a lifelong message for him. First, they assured him that the spirit of his culture was unbroken. Second, what happened that night taught him that his survival also depended on understanding the graciousness of spirit and wisdom of the elders who visited him so that he too might carry on the values of his culture. He is not to lose appreciation for the sacred and mysterious nature of life, nor is he to lose the spirit of generosity that embodies a cultural outlook based in connectedness, interrelatedness, and empathy. The values of the dominant culture, presented here as indifference, isolation, and the thought that every man has to make it on his own by his own efforts, are starkly juxtaposed against the philosophy of trust and humility engendered in this story. His ability to overcome his own doubts about the veracity of the event demonstrates his ability to overcome the values he himself has unconsciously absorbed from the dominant culture.

This story is contrasted with the typical man-against-nature story that is a Hollywood hallmark of the dominant culture's hidden (perhaps not so hidden) colonialist ideology. It is clear that Jeremy could not have battled nature and won. The storm overwhelmed him. The situation was hopeless. And yet by relenting, by trusting and accepting kindness, he survived. The storyline is brief and to the point, and yet it carries echoes of cultural beliefs expressed elsewhere, for instance in *Black Elk Speaks*, the narrated autobiography of Black Elk, printed in 1932, which records the observations of a witness to the genocide enacted against the Lakotas in the latter part of the nineteenth century. Black Elk has a vision in which he sees two roads intersecting. The path his people and all kindred relations (including animals) are on leads to starvation, ruin, and the loss of hope. The path of light and spirit is vitally alive and filled with joy. In his vision, he pulls his people from the path of sorrow and restores the center of the nation's hoop.[15]

In another chapter, Black Elk shares information about another visionary who began leading many different Indian nations in the ghost dance. He attends in 1891, and has a vision:

> On the other side of the ridge I could see a beautiful land where many, many people were camping in a great circle. I could see that they were happy and had plenty. Everywhere there were drying racks full of meat. The air was clear and beautiful with a living light that was everywhere. All around the circle, feeding on the green grass, were fat and happy horses; and animals of all kinds were scattered all over the green hills, and singing hunters were returning with their meat.[16]

In this other land he encounters relatives and friends. Like the old couple in Joseph Marshall's story, these people live in harmony and happiness, and the nation's spirit resides with them. This is a sacred place that cannot be profaned or damaged by derision, violence, or other outer attacks on the nation. It is a refuge where humanity remains intact and unaffected in a realm of spirit.

This story and the legacy of Black Elk's visions resonate in some senses with the Dalai Lama's autobiography, written in 1962, entitled *My Land and My People*, which was later adapted to the screen as the movie *Kundun*. The first fourth of the book is filled with comforting images of old Tibet in which the people of Lhasa, the capital, had "more peace of mind than there is in most of the cities of the world."[17] The Dalai Lama presents Tibetan society as one in which people are easygoing, friendly, and deeply religious; a people who love ceremonies and social occasions.[18] There is a sense that the tradition of Tibetan culture reaches far back in a continuous unbroken chain; the influence of history is inseparable from the present.

Individual consciousness has preeminent importance in Tibetan Buddhist cosmology. Our presence on earth in physical bodies is seen as the product of our attachment to material objects and pleasurable emotions, which through ignorance we see as literally real rather than as dream appearances. Liberation comes from clarity of perception. Underlying Tibetan Buddhist theology is a system of belief that vigorously advocates the power of visualization as a tool for self-transformation. Deities known as yidams are visualized in meditative practices, and the spirits of these perfected beings overflow into the visualizers, bringing blessings and an empowered ability to act with kindness and wisdom. When asked if yidams are real, one Buddhist Lama replied, "No, they are no more real than the dream reality we abide in, falsely assuming that it is substantially real."[19] In other words, they are as real as we are. Many people who meet the Tibetan refugees now residing in India have commented that they seem surprisingly well adjusted and cheerful considering the hardships that they have endured. Part of the reason for this may well be their belief in another realm of existence that enables them to see the extreme hardships endured under imposed genocidal policies as just one dimension of life. Another dimension, a refuge, resides beyond the passing events of this single life.

The Dalai Lama states toward the end of his narrative that "beyond the Himalayas, Tibet is like a gigantic prison camp. For them [my people], the only thing I can do is try to see that they are not forgotten.... Tibetans are human." He adds, "My hope rests in the courage of Tibetans, and the love of truth and justice which is still in the heart of the human race; and my faith is in the compassion of Lord Buddha."[20] His last entreaty is a line from a story about a man exhorted to practice religion, not just the outer trappings of rituals, of public religion. The Lama observing him suggests the following, "Turn your mind away from the forms of this worldly life.... Turn *your mind* towards religion."[21] As in Black Elk's account, worldly life is treated as only a superficial reality; another realm, or perhaps another state of being, exists.

In both of these cases, religion provides a haven from persecution in which a sense of self-worth is cultivated, thus creating hope for the future and the possibility of change in a seemingly hopeless political situation. Even the secular refuge found by Joseph Marshall's lost man in the storm is suggestive of an underlying philosophical structure that would allow for such a possibility.

Resistance to oppression, when it is internal and spiritual, can take on a mysterious dimension of being that defies understanding. For Wallace Black Elk, a contemporary writer and traditional Lakota healer and shaman who considers himself a spiritual grandson of Black Elk, resistance is rooted not only in a sense of community but also in supernatural beings and forces that help maintain the link to a historically continuous sense of culture, even in the aftermath of genocide. His writings demonstrate his belief that through humility and openness he is able to be guided and therefore maintain the spiritual understanding of his people and predecessors through a link that defies explanation. In his prelude to a description of how he was arrested, deemed mentally ill by a judge, and ordered to confinement in a mental institution for his shamanic practices, he shares his impressions of the attitudes of American society and legal system toward Indians.

> There was a time when we couldn't talk about these powers. That was back in the 1920's and 1930's. At that time you would get in trouble for saying those things. But after I came back from World War II, I decided to talk about these powers. So one day I got up, and I was tired of this. So I said to myself, "I'm going to get up, and I'm going to tell the world that this Chanunpa [pipe] is sacred.[22]

For this transgression he was "attacked" by Christians, including some of his own relatives, who got a judge's order to have him evaluated by a psychiatrist. He was put in a straightjacket and confined to a cell.

In a short story entitled "Oliver's Silver Dollar," Joseph Marshall suggests that unjustified incarceration of Indians who didn't toe the line was relatively common in the early to middle part of the twentieth century. The story tells of an Indian man's incarceration in a mental institution from 1937 to 1967 because of a social worker's misunderstanding of a statement he made about the origin of a silver dollar framed on his wall. He was a man who spoke little English and who had been wandering the countryside living as Indian a life as possible until he inherited money and land. The social worker, jealous of his good fortune, angry that an Indian had ready money and self-sufficiency, demanded to know how he got the coin. He answered that he had made it. She took it as a sign that he thought he could fashion it himself from metal and was therefore insane.[23]

It took thirty years for the wrong to be redressed, thirty years for anyone to even bother to ask him for an explanation. "Those who knew him best will tell you that his sanity was never in question. Thirty years of his life was spent behind cold brick walls and an eight-foot-high fence because of his choice of words."[24] He was confined because of stereotypes and an unfounded judgment that he was reclusive and simple-minded.[25] To his judgers, his life was nothing. But for him, the years passed slowly. The woman he was to have married waited for him.

In Wallace Black Elk's account, which is autobiographical rather than fictional, he reports that he was arrested and then confined to a padded cell in a mental institution because of his religious practices.[26] Like Marshall's character, he is confined for who he is seen to be within the worldview of his oppressors. But his sense of freedom comes from another source. While in his cell, a voice speaks to him. He is not afraid. He is at home with spirit guides. The voice says, "Don't worry. Pray. Don't cry. Pray."[27] It is an often-heard suggestion, telling him, as he had been told before in his life, to trust, to put his faith in something beyond the obvious, to fear no obstacle. He reports, "This same spirit always came and consoled me. 'I'm here. I'm a spirit. I'm here to help you. So don't worry. All the things you have been talking about are true.'"[28]

The spirit then brushes past him and opens the cell door. They proceed down a hall together and out of doors. It is night. They look at the stars and moon. There is crusted snow on the ground. Another spirit descends from the clouds and converses with the first spirit, who has left footprints in the snow alongside Black Elk's. He reports, "So I was standing there and looking around—breathing and enjoying what all was around me. It was really good to take a breath and see all what Tunkashila had created and what Grandmother had given me." The attendants at the hospital then catch up with him and demand to know who let him out.[29] Later, after a sweat lodge ceremony is held for him, a gourd visits and tells him he will be released. He is.[30] It is not the decision of his captors. He does not appease them or even try to gain their mercy. He is sustained from elsewhere, and part of that sustenance comes from the community of people around him, such as those who hold a sweat lodge for him, and part of it comes from another source that reaches beyond time and human dimensions.

Black Elk's account is by no means an anomaly. His story is congruent with the cultural beliefs and attitudes with which he was raised. As a boy, his older relatives, recognizing his potential as a shaman, protected him and kept him, illegally, out of public school. He was secluded and hidden away in a space outside the dominant culture. In that culture's interpretation, he was just crazy, nothing more. He was summarily dismissed by people who were outsiders. But when he claimed his own space and became the insider, those who inhabited the dominant culture became the outsiders.

Black Elk is not alone in sharing his experiences with spirit guides who hold the traditions of his people and sustain him in troubled times. Mable McKay, whose story is recorded by Greg Sarris in *Mable McKay: Weaving the Dream*, is likewise sustained by a connection to a spirit guide who teaches her to weave baskets and heal people. Her account is notable in that in her community of Potter Valley, Pomo Indians of California had dispersed by the time she was born. She was raised alone, by her grandmother, who taught her the language. She is guided by visions that come during a period of unconsciousness and fever as a child. The events of her life—working at various low-paying jobs, marrying, living among different communities of California Indians—seem secondary, almost a shadow of the real events of her narrative, which have to do with revelations passed down by the spirit guiding her. She is a visionary. She leads and helps others. But even in the marginally intact communities she encounters, the outer sacred rituals fade under the cultural colonization of Christianity, and much of her spiritual life seems to be interior, except for her influence on individuals such as Greg Harris, who seek her out.

Like Wallace Black Elk, Mable McKay is vibrantly connected to another level of reality, even when Christianity and assimilation wrests her community from its own sacred ways. Her connection to tradition is beyond explanation, and yet it exists. Her baskets are displayed in the Smithsonian Institution as examples of authentic Pomo weaving, and yet it is a spirit that taught her and a spirit that sustained her. She tells the man recording her story, "Spirit show me everything. Each basket has Dream."[31]

Like Black Elk, she seems to be a person who is something more than merely a product of modern times. Unlike Wallace Black Elk, who as a child was recognized as a person destined to be a shaman and was accepted by elders in the community, Mable McKay grew up without even the support of the scattered Native American communities in the area. Many people saw her as an odd child, thin, sickly, who stared quietly and mumbled in her sleep, and they were afraid of her. Steeped in influences from Christian missionaries and science, they interpreted Mable's connection with the spirit world as a sickness rather than an attunement to another realm. Her grandmother was an exception, but she gradually grew too old to care for her.[32] Mable's inner life was left entirely to her, which created a schism between the two worlds in which she dwelled: Indian versus white, traditional versus modern values, and dreamworld versus the alienating isolation of contemporary mainstream society. Somehow she survived the growing divide of two sides of her life and was also able to rescue Greg Sarris, who met her as a teenager lost in apathy and lack of direction. Later, as an adult, he recorded her story.

Her courage is striking. As a young girl, during a sick spell that kept her out of school, she experienced the following:

> "You listen to me," the voice was saying. "I'll teach you. You don't tell nobody what I'm telling you. You don't ask them questions about it. You're being fixed to be a doctor."... But what the spirit was showing her didn't seem good. She saw blood, poison. Ugliness. People carrying bones from the dead, grinding the remains of the orange-bellied newt, weaving the woodpecker's feathers into sun baskets. Bodies swollen and distorted, discolored. Bodies with black growths like roots. Crying. Misery. Hatefulness.[33]

Fearing for her safety, Mable's grandmother brought her to a Moki [healer] of a neighboring Wintun community. He became enraged during a public dance and burned the girl with a coal. She was unhurt; the grandmother worried that he was offended. Instead she was told that the Moki was telling the people that the ceremonies were not being upheld in the right way by the people because times had changed.[34] At age fifteen, Mable was visited by a shaman named Albert who descended in a chariot from the sky in front of a witness, another teenage girl who was walking beside her. He told her to come with him and extended his hand. She refused, saying that the white woman she lived with would not let her go. The very real contemporary world endangered her spiritual development. Albert, in fact, told her she would die in nine months because she refused his offer. The formless spirit who was her guide consoled her and assured her that Albert was another doctor and was merely confused.[35]

Mable was forced to have faith beyond all outward circumstances. Later she was taught by the spirit that she was to heal with baskets. "You make a basket to spit out the sickness you suck with your mouth. Your throat has already been fixed, given. That extra tongue can catch the sickness and stop it. You catch it in your throat, then spit it out."[36] Even her tongue existed in two worlds, both of which had a hold on her and made demands. Later she acquired a clapper and a rattle to aid in curing ceremonies and was publicly recognized as a healer.[37] During the next years, Mable travelled and lived in various communities, some Indian, some predominantly white. She held a series of jobs and eventually worked in a factory.

Another example of the split world in which she lived occured after she met another healer named Essie. The two became very close and Mable joined her in leading ceremonies in a Kashaya community. But Mormon missionaries eventually split the tribe by calling the Indian practices devil worship. Mable described the aftereffects: "The last close-knit traditional Pomo community crumbled. Family against family, sister against sister." The roundhouse, where ceremonies took place, grew less and less full. In addition, "Doors were locked, shutters pulled completely down. Arguments."[38] Essie then informed Mable that her (Essie's) time of death was approaching and instructed Mable to lock the roundhouse because the practices had deteriorated and the next true visionary to lead the Kashaya would be a long time coming.[39] Mable realized that the end of an era had arrived when she heard of plans to build a dam above the riverbed where she collected reeds for her baskets:

> Essie told her about her dream. "They're going to build a dam here one day soon. Where we're sitting will be hundreds of feet under water. This last good sedge-picking place will be no more." Mable knew to believe Essie, just as she knew to believe what Essie said about her own end on earth, about locking the roundhouse. But sitting there in the afternoon spring sun, Mable felt something timeless, endless, something familiar and forever about digging roots by the water with another woman.[40]

It seems like Mable McKay lived at the end of the time that was capable of supporting and recognizing the existence of the complex cosmology of her people. The community was disintegrating. The natural habitat that supported her traditional art was being destroyed. And yet a timeless quality of spirit, a tangible essence that was both memory and presence, extended infinitely.

In the last years of her life, Mable McKay lived in a small city in northern California. She gained some notoriety and began to give lectures at colleges. On one occasion, while being interviewed by a group of psychiatrists and academics, she recalled a story that sounds remarkably similar to Wallace Black Elk's account of his escape. She described a "medicine man who got out of jail by turning into a fly or humming bird." When asked if she believed the story, she replied that she did not, but added, "I believe he went down the toilet."[41] As much as the investigators might have been trying to encapsulate her worldview, they could not. She not only transcended their assessment, she also unhitched their own firm grasp on reality. Her very existence, in fact, rendered their outlook narrow and naive. She, like both Black Elk and Wallace Black Elk, suggested that the reality held as seemingly obvious by dominant, white-influenced culture is an incomplete and flawed version. Even if it holds sway at the moment, its truths are not ultimate.

The tables are turned on the dominant viewpoint when those who are forcibly silenced refuse to comply and reemerge again and again in persistent presence. In *I Know Why the Caged Bird Sings*, Maya Angelou shares countless insights into the varied mechanics of survival. In many ways literature can carry a discussion to greater depths than a speech or a theoretical article, especially when strong social commentary is combined with attention to the minute details of the lives and emotional worlds of characters. Maya Angelou's writing style is superbly intimate. There seem to be no secrets she hides from the reader, who becomes her intimate associate in the close, autobiographical tone she sets.

Ties to tradition and history are alive, at least in spirit, for the young narrator Maya through her connection to "Momma," her paternal grandmother. Momma is a profoundly Christian woman who is embarrassed by emotional displays for other than religious reasons. Her Christianity, like that of other members of her closely knit African-American community, is uniquely connected to her circumstances, as evidenced by an open-air religious revival Maya carefully describes. Everyone excitedly anticipates the event. Maya watches from behind Momma's store counter as tired people return from work: "Their overalls and shirts seemed to be torn on purpose and the cotton lint dust in their hair gave them the appearance of people who had turned gray in the past few hours."[42] Yet they eagerly rush home to clean up for the revival meeting.

Maya observes them and sympathetically asks where they find the energy when the struggles of the day have left them utterly spent. "Go to church in that cloud of weariness? Not go home and lay those tortured bones in a feather bed? The idea came to me that my people may be a race of masochists and that not only is our fate to live the poorest, roughest life but that we liked it like that."[43] She admires their unfathomable reserves of fortitude and indefatigable strength of spirit, and their ability to "shuffle off the cloak of work and the skin of despair."[44]

At the revival, the minister chooses a topic for a sermon that is specifically aimed at his audience. He calls it the "The Least of These," and speaks first about the need to be charitable beyond measure without the least thought of return or thanks, a philosophy Maya's grandmother holds dear. He then continues with a pointed social commentary:

> "Charity don't say, 'Because I give you a job, you got to bend your knee to me.'" The church was rocking with each phrase. "It don't say, 'Because I pays you what you due, you got to call me master.' It don't ask me to humble myself and belittle myself. That ain't what charity is."[45]

His sermon seems to reiterate the vibrantly present personality of Maya's grandmother. One could also say that she personifies the minister's message, for she is a humble and generous woman, but she is not humble before bigots and other arrogant fools. She is humble before God, her God, who is not a white man's God passed down secondhand to her, no...her God. And of the audience Maya relates:

> Their faces shown with the delight of their souls. The mean white folks was going to get their comeuppance. Wasn't that what the minister said, and wasn't he quoting from the words of God himself? They had been refreshed with the hope of revenge and the promise of justice.[46]

They are convinced that they just have to endure and things will become better in the future. They have hope in the possibility of a better world, and this hope sustains them. Maya is aware that "no one would have admitted that the Christian and charitable people were happy to think of their oppressors' turning forever on the devil's spit over the flame of fire and brimstone."[47] They were dreaming of revolution, of a world that could change, and in time, their dreams became reality and moved what seemed immovable. Theirs is the "combative spirituality" that Cornel West describes as:

> a sense of historical patience, subversive joy, and daily perseverance in an apparently hopeless and meaningless historical situation. Black cultural practices emerge out of an acknowledgment of a reality they cannot know—the ragged edges of the real, of necessity; a reality historically constructed by white supremacist practices in North America during the age of Europe."[48]

Cornel West's choice of the phrase "the age of Europe" notes the passing quality of the societal structure presently imposed by historically white-supremacist foundations. In his view, not only is black culture located outside the dominant white culture; its very source is rooted in outsiderness—the knowledge of the denial of basic human rights and freedom from economic misery.[49]

In rural Arkansas in the early decades of the twentieth century, Maya's grandmother was a strong, resourceful, and determined woman who nonetheless carried the memories and aftereffects of slavery that were unavoidably present for the people of her community who were treated despicably by whites and who feared violent manhunts, lynchings, castrations, and verbal assaults. Religion is *Momma's* bastion against the omnipresent degradation and violence inflicted by the surrounding white community, as it is for her neighbors and friends. It is a source of pride and a unifying force. The faith of Maya's grandmother is unshakable.

As Cornel West notes, "Black religious practices—the indigenous cradle of African-American culture—were principally an attempt to provide hope and sustain sanity in light of the difficult position of black Americans."[50] The community created their own world, separate and apart from the dominant culture in which whites maintain a myth of superiority over black Americans. Images abound in Maya Angelou's autobiography of exploitation reminiscent of slavery, in fact little different from it. Young Maya is greeted daily by a predictable sight:

> Brought back to the store, the pickers would step out of the backs of trucks and fold down, dirt-disappointed, to the ground. No matter how much they had picked, it wasn't enough. Their wages wouldn't even get them out of debt to my grandmother, not to mention the staggering bill that waited on them at the company store.[51]

Maya Angelou intends the images she shares to resonate with images of slavery in order to show that much had remained unchanged and that the brutal legacy of past enslavement weighed down the future prospects and daily lives of the black community of Stamps, Arkansas. Struggle for survival was an ordinary experience, as was a sense of pervasive despair that all the effort expended—superhuman effort, fortitude, and patience—was still not enough to make ends meet financially and still not enough to earn respect as intelligent and capable human beings in the eyes of the petty and mean-spirited white community. Maya Angelou criticizes this gross lack of generosity harshly; the white people in Stamps seem incapable of feeling empathy or respect that crosses racial boundaries. For example, the hypocrisy of the white dentist who refuses to treat Maya's cavity because he considers a black mouth unclean is all too evident in light of the fact that he is in debt to Maya's grandmother for money she lent him during the depression. Her generosity of spirit stands in stark contrast to his meanness. In sharing this incident, Maya Angelou leaves no doubt about whose actions and general character are superior in terms of maturity and inner greatness.

Maya withstands the storm of abuse and still stands tall. In fact, in this case, she leaves the office with ten dollars to cover the expenses of traveling to another dentist in a distant city. The words from her famous poem "I Shall Not Be Moved" come to mind, as they do with regard to the incident in which uncouth and disrespectful white children chide Maya's grandmother in front of her store. "Before the girls got to the porch I heard their laughter crackling and popping like pine logs on a cooking stove. I suppose my lifelong paranoia was born in those cold, molasses-slow minutes... Then one of them wrapped her right arm in the crook of her left, pushed out her mouth and started to hum. I realized that she was aping my grandmother."[50]

Her grandmother stoically abides their insults, never expressing anger toward them. She stands unshaken by their onslaught, humming a hymn to herself, even when one of the girls does a handstand and reveals her uncovered genitalia. Her grandmother endures the chastisement and remains determined to be untouched by it. In her mind, the measure of success is the ability to sustain a presence of mind congruent with her religious values rather than lose herself to anger, even when it is justified.

The legacy of enslavement is never far out of reach in *I Know Why the Caged Bird Sings*. It is a burden that, like the cage, marks a circumscribed freedom—the difficult circumstances of economic enslavement and overt racism that form the milieu in which Maya and the residents of Stamps must find their peace, their fulfillment, their happiness and self-respect. Choosing to sing, the vibrantly alive and undefeated bird expresses a spirit of life that cannot be shattered. Maya Angelou captures the circumstances and spirit of the times that led eventually to the civil rights movement of the 1960s.

Theorist Barbara Smith speaks of the way memories of the history of oppression come to the surface and resonate each time a new act of racial hatred must be endured. Referring to the case of Abner Louima, a black Haitian man viciously assaulted and nearly killed by white, male, New York City policemen in August 1997, Smith calls her response as an African-American woman personal as well as political. The incident, and the subsequent efforts by medical and legal personnel to suppress evidence of what had happened, kept her awake at nights and filled her with a dread that had visited her before:

> Day and night, I was near tears whenever I focused upon what he and his family were going through. The despair and fury I felt were nothing new. Since childhood I have been forced to live this nightmare again and again. In 1995, although I was too little to know what it meant, I learned fourteen-year-old Emmet Till's name when he was lynched in Missis-

> sippi for whistling at a white woman. In 1957, when I was ten, I watched nine Black students attempt to enter Little Rock High School while a mob of screaming white adults attacked them verbally and physically.
>
> In 1963 four Black girls near my own age, Addie Mae Collins, Denise McNair, Carole Robertson, and Cynthia Wesley, were murdered when the Sixteenth Street Baptist Church was bombed in Birmingham, Alabama. More than any of the others, their deaths taught me the measure of my life in the great white scheme of things. Somebody's daughter, somebody's neighbor girl, somebody's child, someone with carefully plaited hair and a crisply ironed blouse, someone whose people saw to it that she got to church every Sunday, someone like me was in the end worth nothing, was a creature to be hunted down, obliterated, and killed.[53]

The vision of childhood Maya Angelou presents in *I Know Why the Caged Bird Sings* is one of trauma but also one of love and appreciation for a haven of peace provided by her grandmother's love and the security of her home life with her grandmother, uncle, and brother. The peace she feels is tarnished by racism, by rape and physical abuse at the hands of her mother's boyfriend, and by poverty and its attendant ailments, which affect her self-esteem and that of the community of Stamps. The ability to cultivate wisdom and compassion is a positive aspect of her self-affirmative, warrior-like response. Suffering can bring about compassion, understanding, and maturity. Being an outsider can bring about a heightened sense of awareness. It is a forced circumstance that demands strength and self-reliance as well as critical analysis. When one is the victim, there is nothing alluring or attractive about a philosophy of indifference.

Maya and her community lived in a different world than that dictated by the whites, because there was no possibility of surviving in that world, on white terms, as a black American. Salaries were not enough to live on. Men were lynched. There was no hope of a professional future. For example, at the grade school graduation, the children were told by white invited speakers that they could be sports players and nothing else. And yet as a community they defied this claim when a small boy, the class leader, led them in the Negro national anthem. They defied the men's dismal decree of their inevitable failure not by shouting them down but by waiting for them to depart and rekindling the knowledge of the strength and hope they had within their own community.

Maya Angelou expresses the view that those who are forced to be outsiders are left to find their own way to values that make their lives richer, more humane, and more vitally alive. A short story from *Wouldn't Take Nothing for My Journey Now* shares the reflections of Aunt Tee, a woman who had worked as a maid for sixty years of her life, on an evening when her white employers, an old couple, ask her to crack open the door of her room so that they might observe the comfort, joy, and hominess of her Saturday get-togethers with three other African-American employees of the house:

> And there they both spoke and won Aunt Tee's sympathy forever.
>
> "Theresa, we don't mean to disturb you..." the man whispered, but you all seem to be having such a good time..."
>
> The woman added, "We hear you and your friends laughing every Saturday night, and we'd just like to watch you. We don't want to bother you. We'll be quiet and just watch."
>
> The man said, "If you'll just leave you door ajar, your friends don't need to know. We'll never make a sound."[54]

The image illustrates the starkness of the old couple's lives. It is as if they are estranged from the very images they have created of themselves for public perusal. In fact, even the title "Living Well, Living Good" speaks of the contrast in the different approaches to life between these individuals from different classes and social positions. The couple lives for show. Their half of the title is grammatically correct and would be the phrase of choice at a formal dinner or gathering. One can almost see starched collars on well-cut suits and the expensive revealing dresses, each original and designer made. The conversation is predictable rather than intimate. It is a show, and the actors' lines are as clearly drawn as the lines of a script. On the other hand, those who "live good" have authenticity on their side. Their gathering is devoid of pretense and one-upmanship. Instead, solidarity, sympathy, and understanding are the glue that makes them a community.

The old couple are vulnerable in this moment, and they are asking for human kindness and pity, which they find. In this encounter, they are not standing above the woman who is their maid, their servant. As an employee, her own interests are often subsumed by those of her employers, as if her life were less important than theirs. And yet she is the one with true wealth, brought to her by her generous nature. In fact, the plight of the old couple peering in on life won them her sympathy rather than her contempt.

The image of the couple peering in on life also reveals the equalizing effect of mortality and finitude. Social status has little sway in this scene, where pretense is brushed aside and one human being is left speaking to another. The pair, now lonely and forlorn, are forgotten and unimportant in the high society in which they must have once bounced about.

Similarly, in a striking image from *I Know Why the Caged Bird Sings*, Maya "accidentally" breaks a china bowl owned by her employer, a white woman descended from southern aristocracy. All that is left in the encounter is two human beings face to face. One is crushed and forlorn, the other defiant and empowered—invincible. They are alone. No outside witness could testify that it wasn't just a clumsy accident. It is a face-off. The woman is in tears, having lost a precious heirloom connecting her to the grandeur and status of the past, to the mantle of white social superiority she feels is her birthright. The confrontation was instigated when she tried to rename Maya, to define her in her own terms.

In the light of Maya's defiance, however, her superiority is no more substantial than the bowl that was dropped and easily shattered. Her supposed superiority is not innate, nor was that of her ancestors. She and Maya have locked horns and she has lost, and no one and nothing outside of herself can rescue her. This is the power of the space that Maya has made for herself. She may exist as an outsider to white wealthy society—the dominant culture—but the space she has made for herself gives her a sense of her own subjectivity and identity. This, in and of itself, disrupts the world of assumed white supremacy every time she encounters it.

Maya's grandmother, and Maya herself, relied on self-created havens that sustained a sense of well-being, as did their community. Like Joseph Marshall's characters, whether lost in a snowstorm or locked in a mental hospital; like Black Elk, whose visions helped sustain the hope of his people; like Wallace Black Elk, who defied those who denied the validity of his spiritual experience; and like Mable McKay, who had to have faith that a spirit being sustained both her and her culture, Maya and her grandmother created a net of safety that they wove around themselves to keep their predators at bay. This process is not mere escapism. It is survival.

Spirituality, whether in the form of a hope for the future, a comfort in present pain, or as a literal connection to a transcendent reality, is a sustaining force that carries a disrupting, revolutionary power to shake things up. The present and past circumstances of oppression no doubt exert their influence, but they are not invincible, and the social order they sustain is not immutable. Like scattered cards in a deck landing in random order, our social structure is dominated by one configuration, but this can certainly change in the future. As for the present, its complexity is not easily encapsulated by oppressors when those who are oppressed speak out. In each moment of speech and awareness, reality is already transformed.

a net of safety that they weave around themselves to keep their oppressors at bay. The process is not necessarily, in itself, survival.

Spirituality, whether in the form of a hope for the future, a comfort in present pain, or as a literal connection to a different reality, is a sustaining force that carries a dirty, subversive, revolutionary power to shake things up. The present and past circumstances of oppression no doubt exert their influence, but they are not immutable, and the social order they sustain is not impregnable. Like scattered cards in a deck landing in random order, the social structure is dominated by one configuration, but this can certainly change in the future. As for the present, its complexity is not easily encapsulated by oppressors when those who are oppressed speak out. In each moment of speech and awareness, reality is already transformed.

CHAPTER 5

Expanding the Parameters of Feminism: Self-healing in Toni Morrison's *Paradise*

If what we need to dream, to move our spirits most deeply and directly toward and through promise, is discounted as a luxury, then we give up the core—the fountain—of our power, our womanness; we give up the future of our worlds.

—Audre Lorde[1]

Paradise opens with the murder of an unarmed cluster of women who live in a commune several miles on the outskirts of a predominantly African-American town named Ruby. Subsequent chapters reveal individual stories of each of the women who were killed. We also learn the stories of the patriarchs and of the women of the town whose allegiances are torn between the two groups. The women of the commune are viewed as dangerous by the town-dwellers not because they are violent or actively planning a dismantling of the power structures upheld in Ruby, but because of the potential they hold to change the attitudes of the wives of the patriarchs. Their influence is strong because they are staunchly independent freethinkers. Each of the women who finds her way to the commune by accident or by poetry has reached a point of dramatic transition in her life. Each has arrived at the last jumping-off point, a tiny space carved out in a terrifying landscape that has rejected, abused, and disregarded her.

Toni Morrison creates contexts that centralize the experiences of each of the women characters; no woman's experience is relegated to the margin. It is not an overturning of racial and gender privilege, but rather a dismantling of it, that Toni Morrison seems to seek. The ambiguity of racial determination is purposeful, according to Toni Morrison's own account on an Oprah Winfrey show. In *Paradise,* she is trying to reach a higher ground where humanity as a whole is accessed at the same time that she acknowledges the roles that race and female identity play in the lives of her characters.

Morrison makes each of her characters significant in *Paradise.* They are subjects and individuals. No one subject is meant to be representative of black experience, white experience, or female experience. Each character has a particular story and history. The difficulty a reader may face in trying to "place" each character is instructive. It is a novel about humanity *and* it addresses African-American experience. Race is present but not definable in its meanings and implications. Each character must first be taken for who she is rather than what she represents. This is perhaps in response to the way critics have read her novels as specifically African American rather than broadly human. She grants her characters the same neutral status granted to white characters in mainstream fiction. She has also created a novel that emphasizes the importance of being a woman and the communication, interaction, and compassion that women can share across many boundaries.

As long as they survive, the women are threatening to the male leaders of Ruby because their claim of autonomy threatens the patriarchy's preeminence. It is precisely in the identification these women embrace as outsiders that they achieve freedom, self-respect, healing, and awareness of a transcendent nature to their existence that defies the degraded position allotted to them in the dominant pervasive culture; in this case, even in African-American culture.

The town of Ruby, like the women's commune, serves as a bastion that holds off the encroachment of the dominant (white, male-centered) culture. The shared community identity is essential to the survival of each of the inhabitants because it provides space for members to explore dimensions of identity that are affirming and filled with possibility. Freedom, however, is circumscribed within the boundaries of what the self-appointed leaders of Ruby will allow. This contrasts sharply with the women's commune, which is open and unruled for the most part, where no one person's interests are easily subsumed under another's. The men of Ruby seem to live in emotional isolation from each other and seem to have a reflective sense of themselves only in connection with measurable external achievements, such as social status or landownership. These men wield financial and political power, but they come to fear the women of the commune who have mystical powers to heal, to intuitively divine the future, and to survive by letting go into the flow of life rather than by attempting to rule and direct it.

Mavis, one of the commune residents, has a spiritual quality that at first glance seems to be absent from her day-to-day endurance of misery. She is surviving physically, barely, when she uncovers a vitality inside her, a life within. We first see her as a woman despised by everyone—her boyfriend, her children, her community. The local papers branded her as an irresponsible mother when she accidentally killed her baby twins by locking them in a hot car on a summer day. Even before this happened, though, she was despised. She was everyone's doormat.

Poor and desperate, she steals her boyfriend's car and money from her mother to drive across the country. Mavis is victimized, but we live in a society where victims are seen as hideous and to blame for their own misery. Who cares for Mavis? Who loves her? No one. Her role as mother was to be unquestionably giving and loving, but no one gives her love back. Her partner is brutal in his lovemaking. On the evening of her departure alone into the night, she is in bed with Frank. Frank's sexual relationship with her illustrates the distance between them:

> Mavis relaxed, permitted herself a sigh that she hoped sounded like a snore. The sheet was off before she could complete it. When he pulled her nightgown up, he threw it over her face and let that mercy be ... He didn't penetrate—just rubbed himself to climax while chewing a clump of her hair through the nightgown that covered her face. She could have been a life-size Raggedy-Ann.[2]

When he covered her face, she became an absence, a reality she accepted because she believed him.

Her children pick up on his attitude and feel superior to their mother. They pinch her and take from her but never give. There is even a suggestion that they may kill her for her crime of negligence, although whether her perception of this intent is accurate is left an open question, since the book is written in typical Morrison form as a conglomerate of perspectives minus an omniscient narrator to determine the relative reliability of different views. The accuracy with which this style conveys the confusion and qualified knowledge of everyday life provides one of the aspects that makes her writing vibrant, thrilling, and occasionally disturbing.

At dinner Mavis observes an interaction between her daughter and her daughter's boyfriend: "Sal had Frank's old shaving razor unfolded by her plate and asked her father a series of questions, all starting with 'Is it sharp enough to cut...?' And Frank would answer, 'Cut anything from chin hair to gristle,' or 'Cut the eyelashes off a bedbug,' eliciting peals of laughter from Sal." Mavis silently considers the meaning of their discussion: "She didn't think it would take them long, and seeing how they were at supper, enjoying each other's jokes and all, she knew Frank would let the children do it."[3] Everyone blames her as unnatural and hideous, and as a result she cannot face the monumental woman's task of always being loving and giving and unselfish.

And yet Mavis is a living being. She does not realize the reserves of energy within her at first, but at least she has the will to survive and the energy to escape, to drive to freedom in hastily borrowed rubber galoshes too small for her feet. Is she pitiful or heroic? It all depends. Once she hits the open road, she runs for freedom like a wild animal accidentally let loose from a cage. Her escape plan is to race to open country and endless highways, never looking back toward the past that would drag her down.

Before she escaped, Mavis was an outsider on the margins of existence. She had no support and no place of her own in which to reside. She was an outsider even to her own life, which seemed to run its course regardless of her regrets. But all that changes when she leaves her old life and explores new directions in the women's haven she happens upon. Outsider status empowers the women of the commune and they revel in their freedom, answering to no one, sometimes not even to each other. Life in the commune allows them simply to break off from reliance on the judgments of others. They live in their own world, however circumscribed it may be, and find there a sense of empowerment. The arrival of each woman at the commune and her decision to remain there are influenced by forces of circumstance and intuition. There is a magical quality to their lives, as if the past has been erased, and like children they are free to explore the dimensions of their identities. If these women are dangerous to the men of Ruby it is because they are no longer under the jurisdiction of men.

Gigi arrives in town on a bus, having traveled in search of elusive images of mystical and enduring love. Seneca arrives having left a boyfriend in prison, and other women arrive. None of their origins are as closely laid out as Mavis's, but with each woman there is a sense of running from the past, of running from a life that has spun out of control. Their lives were out of control because they were women whose lives were largely dictated by the needs of others. Only in the commune can they reclaim their own ground and explore their identities.

That the women can survive outside the domain of male authority makes no sense to the men. It speaks to them of a frightening power, one capable of drawing even their own women from their suffocating grasp. What do the women on the commune have to offer their wives?

The best answer to that question may come from Audre Lorde's essay "Uses of the Erotic." She states:

> There are many kinds of power, used and unused, acknowledged or otherwise. The erotic is a resource within each of us that lies in a deeply female and spiritual plane, firmly rooted in the power of our unexpressed or unrecognized feeling. In order to perpetuate itself, every oppression must corrupt or distort these various sources of power within the culture of the oppressed that can provide energy for change. For women this has meant a suppression of the erotic as a considered source of power and information within our lives.[4]

Lorde writes that we need to consider all forms of oppression in terms of not just their political effects but in terms of their spiritual and psychological effects as well. She states:

> The principal horror of any system which defines the good in terms of profit rather than in terms of human need, or which defines human

> need to the exclusion of psychic and emotional components of that need—the principal horror of such a system is that it robs our work of its erotic value, its erotic power and life appeal and fulfillment.[5]

The women of the commune create a space in which infinite possibilities unfold. To the men of Ruby, their matronly abilities to cook and heal, to be sustained by the land rather than by the strength of a man's arm, make the women of the convent witches.

From Audre Lorde's perspective, it might be said that these women are discovering, in seclusion from the onslaught of patriarchy, the power that has been previously suppressed, but not vanquished from, within them. Their seclusion is short lived and ends in their murder, as we learn in the book's beginning, and this is no surprise. They had not hoped to overthrow patriarchal oppression. They merely hoped to run away from patriarchy, to hide from the men who would punish them for their audacity.

Is this the face of modern feminism? The right to abortion is being eroded, lesbians struggle for custody rights over their children, the wages of women are still significantly lower than the wages of men, we have had devastating setbacks in affirmative action policies, and poverty is increasing rapidly in our country. Do any of us still maintain a hope of great transformation, or are we weighed down, frightened, and hiding from confrontation, hoping to hold on to the now-eroding rights won in previous battles? Are all of us running scared or hidden away in havens we think shelter us from the storm to come?

Toni Morrison's novel warns that the forces of oppression are strong and that as women we need to watch our backs. We need to organize, to be visible, and to stay connected to our society. She points out that when we seek seclusion we become vulnerable to the avenues of attack open to the men in power. Whether it is done with fists or guns or laws, the power wielded by the patriarchy cannot be ignored. If we ignore it, it will catch up with us.

On the other hand, Toni Morrison's message may also be that we are more powerful and more threatening to the patriarchy than we realize. Our challenges, even in defeat, break down the seemingly cohesive rationality of the ruling patriarchy. Morrison's writing offers the possibility that patriarchy will collapse in its own vacuity, its lack of profound ideology beyond the claim to inherited privilege. Regardless of their history of enslavement and the injustices they faced in the past, the men of Ruby choose to identify instead with their ancestors' oppressors by basing their identities as men on overbearing masculine privilege and authority. In a sense their positions in terms of race and gender are at war; they choose the privileges of gender rather than acknowledging the victimization of their ancestors on the basis of race. They grasp authority and deny vulnerability. In fact, they shoot it down, especially when it feels too close to home.

The patriarchs of Ruby are terrified. The men have absorbed values that belittle humanity, focusing instead on material gain and status. They become indifferent and inhuman, unfeeling in their actions. In the first chapter, the men, like the Puritans of Salem, hunt down the women who have taken refuge in an abandoned playboy mansion-turned-convent with a cold-blooded, eerie sense of distance from their own actions. They fear the outcast women whose identities do not fall into the pattern of domestic allegiance, quiet endurance, and obedience. These women, by their very existence, prove that they can survive without the gifts and discipline of the masters and so undermine the belief system that makes the patriarchs' authority possible.

That the patriarchs rule by terror is a given, but they prefer to hide that fact from themselves, as if their power were self-created. At the moment of slaughter they view the women as "Bodacious black Eves unredeemed by Mary," not as women who have liberated themselves. They see them as aberrations to be cut away like diseased flesh. And so, "God at their side, the men take aim. For Ruby."[6]

The patriarchs of Ruby hold a conflicted philosophy. They uphold their own autonomy and self-sufficiency as a virtuous tradition handed down by lauded and courageous grandfathers who resisted racial oppression, but they also assert the right to oppress women. In fact they base their sense of self-esteem and comfort not just on their possession of the right to autonomy but also on the illusion of controlling and directing the world around them. Ironically, their heroic resistance to historical colonization and the bonds of slavery is what makes them feel like men, but their image of manhood empowers them to be the same kind of men as the overseers and colonizers who enslaved their ancestors.

bell hooks suggests the concept of power over politics to describe the relationship between those who wield the economic and political power and those subject to the social and legal landscape which they shape. From this framework of understanding it becomes clear that although power dynamics seem to be present in race and gender patterns, these patterns are not innate. They are established through violent acts of domination. Such acts are not acts of strength; they are acts of desperation.

Living in a reality based on principles and public appearance, Steward, one of the men who leads the attack, lives a life of suppressed emotions. He sees himself as a mythic cowboy figure; in his mind, each of his actions is the stuff of legend. His manliness depends on absolute adherence to the image of tough bravado; it allows no humanizing sentiment that might weaken his convictions. He not only eschews the erotic, he actively engages in repressing it. He embraces a notion of masculinity as whiteness in the sense of red, white, and blue American values. In a telling encounter he remembers returning from war and seeing two white men beating an African-American woman who was obviously a prostitute. He fought them, but felt contempt for the woman and realized that "he did not sympathize with the white men, but he could see their point, could even feel their adrenaline, imagining the fist as his own." He wanted that same feeling of power, and eventually he got it.[7]

The community of women that emerges among the seemingly unrelated female characters of *Paradise* seems to be the effect of fate and forces beyond immediate understanding, but their common ground is a need for refuge from the violence and domination of men. Even though the killers "shoot the white girl first," the history of oppression the black women of the convent/haven share with the men who are about to kill them does nothing to protect them from the wrath of men who feel denied their privileges of masculine rule. The men need two things to surround themselves with glory and a sense of significance—to be admired by their women, children, and other subordinates, and to be mythologized in history.

The men of Ruby want to create a history for themselves because they see an obvious gap between the status of white men and their own status. White historical accounts erased all marks of their presence and rootedness in history. They remember their own history and feel great pride in their all-black town that was founded through the sweat and sacrifice of their newly emancipated ancestors. The symbol of the patriarchal mantle they claim as their heritage, and the touchstone of their authority and weightiness in their community, is a communal brick oven whose cast-iron door has a cryptic inscription, "Beware the furrow of his brow." They take this to mean "Fear God, fear authority, and watch your step."

The men's vision of themselves is fixated on a view of the world conducive to enhancing their importance and scope of influence. They feel trapped in a subordinate position in a social hierarchy that devalues blackness, just as it devalues women. They wish to disassociate themselves from the women they look down upon as vulnerable and weak. It is almost as if the murder of the women represents for them an exorcism of their own vulnerability, as if they are exorcizing their own pasts when they murder the women of the convent. Although they publicly extol the virtues of the ancestors who built their town, they are silent about the time before, when the ancestors were enslaved and brutalized. They are enraged by that past, by the unbearable necessity to submit to authority so obviously in the wrong. As they kill the women, they beat back the pain of humiliation that they cannot shake even with their social prominence and economic success.

They want to see death, to cause it with their own hands. It is a last-ditch effort to feel alive, to keep their own lifelessness at bay. They try to fill an aching hole by obliterating all signs that anything more was ever possible. They have accepted the white man's definition of manhood, one based on oppression, dominance, brutality, and an absence of emotion.

When masculinity is established through power and dominance over others, masculinity itself can become racialized; power dynamics become the means of defining, qualifying, and establishing masculinity, and these dynamics are acted out in a variety of arenas. The compulsion to dominate takes on varied forms. To rule, to be the ultimate man in this warped sense, it is necessary to reside at the apex of every conceivable social hierarchy, to submit to no one. Dominance, rather than autonomy, becomes the goal, and the only path to this sort of victory is to vanquish all challengers. It is a brutal picture.

Although it is conceivable that gender could be neutral, just as race could be neutral, in our culture these biological realities are loaded with values and privileges, and the men of Ruby use them to seek power, privilege, and revenge. The women of the commune, who represent abstract and archetypal womanhood, become a force beyond their control. To the men they symbolize witches, mothers—women whose sensuality fascinates and overwhelms them, whose beauty intoxicates, and whose intelligence acts with or without their sanction. They have no choice but to kill or admit defeat, and these proud men will never admit defeat.

Instead, the men take the easy way out; they assume that their dignity is already established as if automatically consecrated by God. They fall back on imagined privilege and give up truly living as individual human beings.

The humanity of the women survives the slaughter, even if they themselves do not. The women live on, their spirits intact. Mavis, for example, revisits her daughter Sally to explain herself to her. She describes that she couldn't come back into their lives because there was no space for her there to survive and breathe. She orders food in the restaurant where she and her daughter are briefly reunited. The emotions of this spirit/human encounter are simple and comforting, direct and unhindered:

> Sally picked up a fork, slipped it into her mother's plate, scooping up a buttery dollop of grits. When the fork was in her mouth, their eyes met. Sally felt the nicest thing then. Something long and deep and slow and bright.[8]

The two reflect that they shared a commonality in their lives together, abused by the same man. As a child, Sally did not respect or defend her mother, but as an adult she can see their similarities, and can see that her mother was not responsible for the abuse her boyfriend dealt her. Like the men of Ruby, she had tried to disassociate herself from the disempowered, vulnerable state she felt her mother occupied. In a supremely feminist moment, mother and daughter find common ground and realize that although women can turn against each other, they can also overcome that pattern and bond with each other. It is a moment of resolution imbued with the hindsight that grants perspective once the finitude of each position is made evident. Mavis is a ghost. She has already died. But she lives on in connection to those who remember her. The boundaries of life and death are not delineated in this last section. It is not clear who, if any, of the women might have physically survived.

Each of the women, before and after life, is engaged in a journey that is unfathomable but that reveals itself over time. Each is led by particular circumstances to a haven outside the world that caused them pain.

Morrison offers glimpses at the afterlives of other women in the novel. Gigi, Seneca, and Pallas each revisit family members after their deaths. Theirs is a freedom unimaginable to their killers. Their lives and their deaths are sacred passages that cannot be desecrated or stolen.

Morrison examines the question of how to proceed from a place of ruin, destruction, and death. It is a timely issue. Those who can rely on inner strength, compassion, and love, as do the women of *Paradise,* live within a shining light. Although their fate in the novel is death, in life they had begun the process of recovery from pain and destruction. In contrast, their killers have lost their humanity. Despite the scenes of violent murder that bookend the novel, *Paradise* is a story of hope. The women of the novel move beyond mundane materialistic striving into the realm of the spirit. And at the end of the novel, an afterlife emerges that cycles back to where it began and moves ever forward.

CHAPTER 6

The Transformative Power of Personal Voice: Students' Rights to Free Expression

When someone with the authority of a teacher, say, describes the world and you are not in it, there is a moment of psychic disequilibrium, as if you looked into a mirror and saw nothing. Yet you know you exist and others like you, that this is a game with mirrors. It takes some strength of soul—and not just individual strength, but collective understanding—to resist this void, this non-being, into which you are thrust, and to stand up, demanding to be seen and heard.

—Adrienne Rich[1]

I have decided to include an essay on teaching strategy in the hopes of answering the question that always arises from theories of social justice—"OK, so now what? Knowing what we know now, how do we change the world? How do we put our philosophies into action?" Part of that answer, for me, has involved contemplating the possibilities and limitations of the college classroom as a site of feminist, cultural, and personal empowerment. The two largest dilemmas in my classrooms have been accepting the role of authority expected of me while cultivating a sense of self-confidence and self-determination in the students, and at the same time creating an atmosphere of freedom that allows for lively, heartfelt, and open discussions while maintaining guidelines of expected courtesy and mutual respect.

These two expectations—the decentering of authority and the cultivation of free expressive voice—are the products of years of study as a graduate student in many and varied feminist classes. As a feminist and humanist, one of my primary goals as a teacher is to help students understand that there are many voices and views available to them to help them build a worldview adequate to the task of addressing the social conditions that affect our communities, our country, and our world. I want them to leave my class understanding a little more about the significance of their own views and life circumstances and how their perspectives intermingle with others. I want students to realize they have voices. I want to them to use their voices. I want them to think about how their own experiences give them insight into the works of fiction and theory we read. I want them to think about what they have read as an inspiration to write, create, and share their own deeply significant stories and visions.

In the call for papers on the topic of "personal voice in teaching" in the Summer 1998 Modern Language Association newsletter, I was struck by one of the questions posed: "How personal should we *expect* students to become?" In my experience as a teacher at Binghamton University I have come to feel that the question is rather "How personal should we *allow* our students to become?" For me, the answer is clear. We should allow students to become intensely personal in their writing. But we should also push them to be intensely critical and analytical about their personal experiences; they should be able to connect them to relevant materials they read in our courses. These topics include social dynamics such as gender, race, and class relationships as well as psychological issues. My reasoning is simple: the level of sophistication and maturity in my students' writing has corresponded directly to their interest and excitement in sharing observations that reflect their authoritative knowledge of particular aspects of life in the United States and beyond.

Discussions in my classes often seem to move between interpretation of the texts and observations that relate to daily experience, and as a result I decided early on to give assignments that allowed students to make the same movements in written form. The permissible range includes anything from a personal response to a passage that a student has carefully set forth and explained, to taking off on a tangent, to a prose narrative, story, or poem that connects to some aspect of the course. Because the classroom environment is oriented toward participation and community building, there are many chances for students to share their works in progress with others and to cooperate in group presentations on works studied in class.

In the first college-level literature course I taught, entitled The Power of Personal Voice in Women's Writing, students read works by Esmeralda Santiago, Dorothy Allison, Leslie Marmon Silko, Leslie Feinberg, Maryse Conde, and Minnie Bruce Pratt. Aside from one rather standard paper requirement, I gave the students free range to respond to questions I raised about the readings in several short paper assignments. Their final assignment, a long paper, was open-ended. They could choose to share their own stories, whether they were fictional or autobiographical, or they could respond to one of the texts we had read in whatever way they chose. For example, they might choose to write a dialogue with the author or discuss a particular issue in the text and connect it to their own personal experiences.

At first I was concerned about criticism from my colleagues and supervisors that I was not serious about teaching the fundamentals of literary analysis and that I failed to clearly distinguish fictional writing from rhetoric and critical writing for my students. But I had to ask myself what I felt good writing was, and (acknowledging that my feelings about writing are highly subjective) I concluded that for me it is a combination of poetic clear prose and significant revelations. It is not a form I can dictate or force on my students. Rather, it is writing that says exactly what each person means to say. It is writing that emerges in an environment in which students are intensely aware that they have important things to say, that they have the urgent need to say them, and that they have the right to speak.

So I took a chance. I told my students that I respected them as intelligent, thoughtful, compassionate, and wise human beings and that I wanted to hear what they had to say. I emphasized that each person in our circle of chairs contributed to the shape of our discussions and inquiries as a group and that I was the designated facilitator. I encouraged students to participate actively in class discussions in a manner that demonstrated respect for everyone present, and to read selected passages from their work aloud, although this activity was optional since some of the topics were extremely personal and I was aware of the need for discretion. I have received papers on students' individual challenges with anorexia, childhood sexual abuse, violent fathers, and racial discrimination in the workplace. Students have also written about the consequences of challenging the cultural values of their first-generation immigrant parents, the detainment and torture of family members in Guatemala, and other moving and serious topics.

One thing that my experience as a teacher has impressed on me is that I am fortunate to encounter so many thoughtful, clear-minded people in my classrooms. I am also lucky to be present in a class where they are invited to share sides of themselves that are often hidden and to voice thoughts on issues central to their lives. Every aspect of the classroom experience links together, and the fact that students speak back and forth readily, sometimes debating, sometimes reinforcing each other's thoughts, contributes to their work as writers in discovering the issues they wish to explore and presenting a logical sequence of arguments and examples to convey their message.

Even though I give my students a great deal of freedom, many still cling to patterns they have learned. They often ask, "What should I write about? What do you want to see in this paper?" I find a veiled complaint in this question: "Why do I need to write about this book? The author's already said it! What is critical writing about anyway?" One student claimed that all literary criticism was nonsense and a waste of time. My answer is always that I understand the need to feel that you are doing something useful—something personally, socially, and even spiritually useful—rather than just fulfilling an assignment. I answer the question of why we engage in literary criticism by suggesting that we undertake *literary engagement* instead; that we ask ourselves what a particular author has said that resonates for us, that spurs us to respond and to remember, to find in our own hearts the reason we need to speak. In "Poetry Is Not a Luxury," Audre Lorde eloquently expresses the beauty and power of finding the words that need to be said:

> I speak here of poetry as a revelatory distillation of experience, not the sterile word play that, too often, the white fathers distorted the word *poetry* to mean—in order to cover a desperate wish for imagination without insight.
>
> For women, then, poetry is not a luxury. It is a vital necessity of our existence. It forms the quality of the light within which we predicate our hopes and dreams toward survival and change, first made into language, then into idea, then into more tangible action. Poetry is the way we help give a name to the nameless so it can be thought. The farthest horizons of our hopes and fears are cobbled by our poems, carved from the rock experiences of our daily lives.[2]

The key goal in a literature classroom that emphasizes personal voice is that students answer the author's thoughts with their own inner wisdom. My way of answering a student's question of what I want from her/him is not to answer. I say, "There is nothing I want you to write. What do you want to write? What do you *need* to write?"

I recently received some positive confirmation of these thoughts when Toni Morrison joined a panel at Cornell University to speak about her novel *Beloved*. Members from a reading group called Sistas Reading Sistas joined her onstage to speak about the ways the book affected them in their thinking about their own lives. One panelist said that certain characters reminded her of some of her relatives. She added that the book had made her think closely about slavery and had made her realize that as an African-American woman she had hidden away awareness of this history because she felt a veiled sense of self-directed shame and knew that she had tried to bury this cultural memory. Toni Morrison responded that no one wanted to remember, neither African Americans nor European Americans. She went on to describe the importance of giving names, voices, and being to those human beings whose stories and lives the dominant record book of history has attempted to erase by considering them nameless.

As I witnessed the fruitful discussion that emerged when the women on the panel shared their personal experiences directly with the author, I realized again the value of literary engagement. Even in writing, it is possible to speak back and forth with an author (especially one as rich in multilayered revelations as Toni Morrison) to call on one's own life and respond, and to listen again for clarification as the discussion builds and sheds light on new ground.

The valuing of the personal voice was evident at this event in several ways. First, Toni Morrison demonstrated how her own writing, though fictional rather than autobiographical, focuses on the personal voice, specifically on giving a personal voice to a figure rendered anonymous by a cold and barren rendition of history. She rewrites a commonly accepted version of history by filling in what had been an erasure. She also fills in erasures in our lives today, because in recognizing the power of those who have passed on, the voices of those still present are empowered. Second, Toni Morrison listened to each of the speakers, each of whom had something to say. Even as I sat in the audience, silently participating, I felt the intimacy of the interactions and the ways in which her readers (and even Morrison) were enriched by the lively discussion, for Morrison is clearly a writer who invites give-and-take. In her speech on an earlier night she suggested that discussion is part of the process that develops the work she has created.

The kind of empowerment that the personal voice enables has multiple repercussions in the classroom as well. The very fact of realizing that one has the right to speak—that one has a voice, thoughts, and experiences that matter—has huge political and personal repercussions, all the more so for students of color or members of any group that is in some way disenfranchised from the hegemonic structures that define American identity. Whether this involves a young Latino man speaking up in class about his anger for having been followed around by security personnel in a department store the previous day, or whether it is a young Korean-American woman expressing her frustration at spending her time in public school grouped with others in an amorphous category called generic Asian Chinese, the stories and voices that emerge from these experiences connect to the same political and personal transformation that is set in motion by many of the works taught in a multicultural literature class. The observations of a European-American young woman about why and how she became anorexic breaks another kind of silence, one that allows systematic violence, oppression, and patterns of self-hatred in women to continue as an endemic disease of modern-day society. (I was shocked in one class when a young white man rudely cut off a fellow student who was connecting the Barbie dolls of her childhood with her current feelings about her body, saying loudly, "Get over it! I played with GI Joe dolls and it didn't affect me!" In thinking how to respond, I realized that such things are not talked about in his world and therefore they do not exist for him, that he wanted to hold on to the world he knew. A long classroom discussion/lecture ensued on what it means to cut off another person and why his words were a form of silencing.)

There are many silences to be broken. The growing presence and recognition of women writers and writers of color, queer writers, and writers who speak about poverty or other injustices disrupt the fantasy image of America fed by television in which all good women are chaste, all white families rich, nuclear, and robustly heterosexual, and all people of color criminals or marginal acquaintances of the main characters. The presence of multicultural literature in at least some English courses provides the possibility for a positive transformation of these widespread media-fostered images, but for such a course to become truly radical, students must participate in the process of personal and cultural inquiry. The voices of students provide the necessary balance that reveals the underlying connections between personal voice as literature and personal voice as a politically charged tool for personal and community transformation.

There are those who feel that a personal classroom is too "touchy feely," that emotions and personal revelations cause discussions to digress and veer away from the content of the course, and there are those who fear the emotional and professional burden of listening to the hardships of their students. One colleague expressed the opinion that she did not consider herself a therapist and refused to allow personal revelations in her class. I also am not a therapist, and I do not attempt to play such a role with my students. I do, however, feel that writing and responding to literature can be a healing process. I also believe that many personal and emotional issues are also cultural issues and have been analyzed and addressed by cultural theorists. As a result, I have on occasion suggested books that match concerns raised by individual students. For example, I have suggested Susan Bordo's *Unbearable Weight* to students who write about anorexia. However, I never assume that any person's writing is anything other than fiction, and I make it clear that this is the case. This gives students the space to write what they will, to experiment, to be free of being hemmed in by literal, ascertainable, and circumscribed truths.

Years ago, a friend of mine was taught in the seventh grade to write in deadpan, technically correct, virtually substanceless school lingo after she turned in a candid essay on her feelings about her parents' divorce. After her teacher referred her to counseling, she vowed never to expose herself to such humiliation again. I am trying to unwork these sorts of negative patterns of writing we have all developed due to institutional pressures, but I am not trying to heal anyone. If people heal themselves, that's their business. I am a listener and a facilitator. When a student came to my office once and told me of the difficulties she was facing with the "F.O.B." Korean community on campus, I listened to her dilemma. She explained that F.O.B. stood for "fresh off the boat," a phrase I had never heard, but which she insisted was common jargon. Apparently, there had been some sort of cultural clash, because although her accent in Korean was perfect, she had lived in the United States for many years and had changed significantly in her social attitudes. She explained that the only people who understood her situation were the few people she knew whose circumstances were similar. Her situation was exacerbated by a feeling of alienation from dominant American culture. My response was to suggest that she write about it, and we discussed together how she might approach such a topic. I never considered counseling her, but listening is another matter altogether.

Another student, a European-American lesbian woman, approached me after class one day to talk about her feelings of alienation from the university lesbian community. We walked to the co-op for a natural root beer, and as we sat on a dilapidated couch together she told me that her feminine appearance led to suspicion among some of her new peers on campus that she was "just trying it out" and "wasn't really a lesbian." I offered to lend her some books and suggested that she might want to respond to one of them for her paper. She chose eventually to respond to *S/HE* by Minnie Bruce Pratt. I expressed empathy for her situation and shared with her some of my own experiences as a non-conformist lesbian who can't even play softball. We discussed at great length the disappointment she felt in finding out that lesbian identity did not equate automatically with open-mindedness and tolerance. In this case I chose to share a part of my life. I did not feel threatened in doing this, and I do not feel that I crossed boundaries that caused discomfort for either of us. It's simply that the relationship of being teacher and student does not preclude the possibility of speaking on equal terms as human beings. In both of the cases mentioned, I facilitated a linkage of issues. My responses were spontaneous, but they emerged from my underlying philosophy about the role of a teacher.

One of the obvious questions I face is how to respond to the personal revelations of student writers. I often respond as a teacher first, saying what I think worked and didn't work as strategies and correcting obvious mistakes or oversights, much as a proofreader would. I write copious comments in the margins and a letter to the student at the end of the paper. Somewhere in that end letter, particularly when a paper has been exceptionally riveting, I respond as a human being. At times I suggest that she/he might consider developing her/his work and publishing it in the future. I stop my own process of second-guessing what a teacher should say, and I say what comes to mind. I express, perhaps, how impressed I am with the clarity of the piece, with her/his courage and integrity as a human being, or simply how I felt as I read it. I remove my mantle of authority and respond because something in what she/he has written touches me. My response corresponds to the level of engagement I encourage students to use when analyzing and responding to the texts and authors we read.

Reading the papers I receive for my open assignments is one of my most exciting experiences as a teacher. Instead of wrestling with students over what an introductory paragraph should look like and what organization and cohesiveness mean, I find myself reading dramatic, moving pieces by writers whose flow and clarity amaze me. I hardly feel as if I am dealing with the same students. Often, several students come forward at the semester's end to express the impact the class had on them. By writing about subjects they cared deeply about, they came to feel like writers. They are.

The most basic tenet of my classes is that the students are already writers. At times, at academic conferences and elsewhere, I have encountered attitudes on the part of well-meaning teachers of literature classes that imply that they are going to shape or create their students as writers. They assert that they are going to make writers out of them. They are going to teach them the form and help them *conform*. I always find this kind of sentiment oppressive, first for the arrogance of it, and second, because although the form hovering over students' heads is never quite identified, it shadows all too closely the exclusivity of the hallowed canon, nestled in the pristine recesses of hoary academe. It is amusing to me that such lofty educators often sigh aloud at the heavy burden they carry, at the impossible task before them, at the responsibility they so nobly take on, to think and become for their students. I personally have no desire to create a writer, just as throughout my life I have resisted being created as a writer and thinker by the educational institutions that have required my disgruntled conformity and compliance from an early age. My task is to facilitate, to encourage students to test boundaries and to stretch out as writers; in short, to become aware of their own vast and explosive power.

To foster a feeling of openness and the sense that our class is a place for artistic endeavor, I often intersperse critical responses with creative writing assignments, utilizing books such as Leslea Newman's *Writing from the Heart*, a collection of creative writing exercises. Reinforcing my view that personal writing is empowering, she states in her introduction:

> NOW HEAR THIS: every woman has important stories to tell and the ability to tell them. There are no exceptions. Not even you.... Writers are not special. Rather, every woman has the potential to be a special writer. This contradicts everything most of us have been taught.[3]

Radical teaching means having the courage to create room to empower one's students, and encouraging personal voice in writing allows room for students to be performers, rather than mere spectators, and for vitality to emerge in the written form. Why shouldn't our writing and our thoughts, the way we spend our days, be vitally important to each of us? Why shouldn't the chance to write be a gift rather than a sullenly accepted assignment in which the writer struggles every moment to second-guess the expectations of her/his judges? Bringing such ambitions to fruition in the classroom not only requires careful selection of authors but also careful consideration of teaching style. In all of my courses, I have followed a philosophy of encouraging students to share their revelations and responses with the classroom community and to see themselves as artists.

I am presently teaching a course entitled Multicultural Women Writers, in which I am covering works by Jamaica Kincaid, Maya Angelou, Toni Morrison, Janice Gould, Leslie Marmon Silko, and Ann-Marie MacDonald. (Although I am unhappy with a course title that singles out women of color as "other," as somehow distinct from "regular" women writers, I wanted to experiment with a phrase that directly indicated that this course would not have a white-dominated reading list.) Last spring I taught a course called Writers of Conscience, which addressed autobiographical works and essays by members of communities faced with overwhelming oppression. In several cases, the authors expressed in their works the need for inner transformation of their own psyches in order to be able to act rationally, compassionately, and effectively in the trying circumstances they faced. We read works by the Dalai Lama, Bette Bao Lord, Audre Lorde, Black Elk, Vietnamese Buddhist nun Chan Khong, and Howard Zinn. In this case, I experimented by asking students not only to respond personally and creatively but also to tie in the perspectives they expressed with the kinds of social critique happening elsewhere in the course.

To understand these works, it was necessary to read background information on Native American history, the Vietnam War, and the passive resistance to racial domination and genocide in Tibet. It was also necessary to have many discussions about the devastating effects, both private and public, of racial oppression in the contemporary United States and about the positive effects of the civil rights movement of the 1960s. In fact, one acquaintance suggested that I was teaching a sociology course. But I feel that literature arising from a sense of social responsibility exhorts all of us to awareness that there is a need for change, to create a just society.

One day I brought in an article about a young African-American man in New York City who was shot by police in a stakeout because they thought the metallic shine of a Three Musketeers bar he was carrying was a gun. He survived to tell the story of the policemen's casual gossip and indifference while they stood over him, offering no aid as he lay bleeding on the ground.

The inevitable questions arose: "Why didn't the popular media cover this event?" "Why should a black man be automatically read as guilty and dangerous?" "How can cops get away with being so indifferent, as if a black man's life isn't very important?" As a result of the class discussions and the inspiration of Audre Lorde, who the class was reading at the time, I received essays that addressed topics such as growing up African American and female in New York City and living as a second-generation Asian American. I also received a creative retelling of the experiences of one student's grandparents in concentration camps during the Holocaust, recountings of personal responses to racism, and purely fictional works relating to different subject positions in American culture and history. I was as moved as my students, because I had *allowed* them to share the richness of their experience and feelings. I never forced anyone to write personally—a standard paper was always welcome and appropriate, but not a single student chose that option on this assignment.

Their writing about their own lives was an integral part of the course, because every previously silenced voice that is heard empowers all of us by decentering the power structures that hold privilege in place. Fostering an awareness of the stories that have not yet been told does not diminish us. I often feel saddened by the canon-worshippers who are blind to their own self-serving attitudes in asserting that classics must deal only with seemingly neutral transcendent human questions and who therefore exclude literature that deals with pressing contemporary issues. Claims that the realm of true literature is somehow more than human and must remain exclusively beyond the reach of living, breathing people in order to avoid devaluing "high" literature echo the sentiment of laws and mores that prohibited miscegenation earlier in this century.

There *is* something transcendent about human suffering, but affirming the kind of compassion fostered by such awareness should not be confused with attempts to "prettify" our national identity by glossing over the overt and covert violence that shapes the daily life and history of our citizens. I believe our goal in teaching multicultural literature classes is broader than merely trying to find a place in the canon for the inclusion of writers marginalized for reasons of class, race, gender, or gender orientation. Writers who continually disrupt the veneer of neutrality in literature are able to do so not because they are women or people of color but because their work looks critically at their positions in the world and forces readers to consider their own positions. In this way literature can actively challenge those who are in positions of authority that circumscribe the rights of others and can empower those who seek freedom from the violence of oppression.

The thing that connects the authors covered in my courses is that their writing could never be termed "neutral" because this term implies a condition of stasis, complacency, and relative comfort with the status quo. The traditional villains in seemingly neutral storylines are often individuals: James Bond's adversaries, the original Terminator, Sadam Hussein, and so on. The villains of the works by revolutionary writers are not only individuals, they are also the power structures that give absolute significance to the will of certain individuals while stripping others of self-determination.

Toni Morrison's novel *Paradise* illustrates this point. In one scene, the young people of the town of Ruby raise up their voices at a town meeting. They defy the elders of the town and challenge a long-held interpretation of a phrase emblazoned on a communal cast-iron oven. Time has obscured its meaning—the inscription is faded and only partly decipherable. There is no way to return to the source to find the true meaning of the phrase, and yet the elders steadfastly assert the sacredness of the master narrative that has dominated their town's history. "Beware the Furrow of his brow," the elders read, and assume in their own minds an unassailable position of authority, aligned with a stern and unforgiving God. "Be the furrow of his brow," the young people assert. They claim the right to self-determination and assert that social categories and inequities are encrusted artifacts of a system that sees itself as innate. But the system always and inevitably is the product of choices to shun social responsibility and rely on the weight of tradition and the status quo. While the elders base their decisions on fear, holding blindly to tradition and the familiar by maintaining whatever hold they have on property or prestige, the young people have a stake in living a life based on the possibility that a just society can be created through careful choice and action.[4]

I include this example because it illustrates the social movements of the 1960s that significantly challenged the white-washed cultural landscape of the United States and paved the way for the emergence and recognition of writers and artists from diverse social backgrounds and a questioning of the sanctity of an exclusive literary canon, among other things. Like the young people of Ruby who would not be silenced in their defiance of figures of authority, the emergence of new literary voices and genres has not been silenced by the stoic resistance of the canon-defenders of "high" culture. At times, in fact, their arguments seem like barely veiled racist, genderist arguments that position their defenders as unassailable literary critics, able to discern at a glance the attributes of "great," "transcendent," and "classic" literature.

A classroom in which multicultural literature is taught is often read as openly and brazenly political, in part because the authors often present challenges to persistent cultural myths that seek to decriminalize the violence that characterizes this country's history and many of the policies, laws, and common biases in practice today. As we watch hard-won civil liberties recede before our eyes—affirmative action, Equal Opportunity Programs, women's rights to self-determination over their own bodies, government assistance of food and shelter for human beings in conditions of need—it becomes obvious that literature functions as more than entertainment for the privileged. Canon-defenders may claim that it is inevitable that the quality of literature will erode without an exclusive hierarchy of greatness. But the fact that women writers, writers of color, and other diverse voices are nearly absent from the canon proves its perpetuation of privilege. In her book *Twilight Zones,* cultural critic Susan Bordo offers a challenge to those who feel that the value of literature will be lowered by the dispersal of a recognized canon:

> Embracing the temporal, provisional nature of our conclusions, analyses, arguments does not entail descent into absolute chaos. In any given situation there are still reasons to believe some accounts over others, to deem some works "greater" than others.[5]

There is a way to measure the value of literature without holding it up to an otherworldly template of completely imaginary, yet unspecified, perfection. One can apply this observation to student writing to argue that it is possible for education to increase the parameters of freedom rather than to contain and control thought. As a teacher, I have no desire to hold up a template to my students, one which presumably only I have the power to read, in order to claim the authority to dictate what good writing is. Of course, there are tools that I have picked up through experience that I can share. There are rules that I have learned, many of which can be broken. I can no more say precisely which rules are essential to good writing than I can enunciate the criteria of what makes certain works of literature profoundly moving or important. A work of literature is more than its pieces, and so is a student's essay.

Movement away from the very concept of a canon seems integral to the construction of a multicultural literature classroom, but the dismantling of the canon remains incomplete as long as the voices of students remain silenced in fear of the authority of our educational institutions. In some sense, students in any classroom who engage in a depersonalized literary criticism remain distanced from the texts and from the authors. It is understood from the very structure of the rigidly hierarchical academic paradigm upheld in most colleges that writers such as Maya Angelou and Toni Morrison are to be viewed as icons rather than as inspirations for the reader's own creative unveiling of stories. In this sense, even though their presence as distinguished authors disrupts archaic notions of the canon, the dismantling is only complete when students can claim these women as their own, can feel such intimacy that they themselves are compelled to voice their own reactions, deeply felt convictions, and creative spirit. When students are encouraged to think about their own opinions and philosophies of life, they often can see a connection between themselves and the authors they read.

As bell hooks states in her essay "Building a Teaching Community,"

> Many teachers who do not have difficulty releasing old ideas, embracing new ways of thinking, may still be as resolutely attached to old ways of *practicing teaching* as their more conservative colleagues. That's a crucial issue. Even those of us who are experimenting with progressive pedagogical practices are afraid to change. Aware of myself as a subject in history, a member of a marginalized group, victimized by institutionalized racism, sexism and class elitism, I had tremendous fear that I would teach in a manner which would reinforce those hierarchies. Yet I had absolutely no model, no example of what it would mean to enter a classroom and teach in a different way.[6]

I share bell hooks's desire for social change, and I feel encouraged and inspired by her bravery in paving new territory as a theorist and teacher. My position in the world is different, but I share many of her goals. Part of my struggle is that even as I abdicate my authority as a teacher I am forced to occupy it, partly for the obvious reason that I am the one to award grades and pass judgment and partly because mine is not a classroom where anything goes. Several times I have felt the tension between my policy that students have absolute freedom to disagree with each other and speak out in class and the reality that this policy sometimes creates situations in which I and other students have been hurt, frightened, and disturbed by the comments that arise. Although I always encourage open and frequent verbal participation in my classes, I have also found it necessary to insist on respectful interactions between students who disagree. I have no desire to censure students, but I do feel that engagement of authors means respecting them as human beings and listening to what they are saying. It often happens, however, that some students are quick to pass judgment on writers based on stances that prevent them from listening, and they are just as quick to pass judgment on their fellow students and on entire communities.

For example, more than once, students have made unconscious, or perhaps conscious, racist judgments of groups of people, based on a superficial understanding of history and present-day circumstances. Some students want to deny the violence of our history. My response almost always is to utilize their challenges by bringing in readings on theory and history that pertain to the topic at hand. I often suggest outside readings to those who are interested. One of the main obstacles to overcoming biased attitudes is a mindset of "us" versus "them," the idea that people who are racially or culturally different from the dominant group are *so* different that it is impossible to communicate with or understand them. It is all too easy for a student who sees him or herself as a member of the dominant group to criticize such people for not conforming to his or her view of life. It happens all the time. Although I don't wish to cover over diverse realities with platitudes such as "we're all the same," focusing on difference and distance rarely seems to foster respect. So I have generally challenged the language used by students that reduces discussion of the circumstances and experiences of human beings to utterly and completely *other*.

As Susan Bordo states in *Twilight Zones*:

> Our students need to be jostled awake from their culture-bound "arrogant perceptions"; they also need, however, to learn the historical origins of those perceptions, the social relations that sustain them, the systems of thought in which they are embedded, and so on. Simply introducing students to different voices is not enough, if only because Western culture has not been a celebration of diversity, and treating it as such cannot explain the actual inequalities of the world we live in.[7]

One of my students, an African-American woman, recently told me during a private meeting that she couldn't discuss race issues out loud in class because it felt too dangerous. (The same student later led a class discussion on race based on passages from Maya Angelou's *Wouldn't Take Nothing For My Journey Now*.) I listened to her words and realized that I too felt frustrated by the insensitive comments of certain students in the class. I did battle the best I could. When one young man suggested loudly that nothing particularly brutal had been done to "Indians," I brought in quotes proving otherwise. When he cut off other students, I tried to rein him in. But even for more open-minded students, discussions pertaining to race often unearth their own racism, bias, and prejudice. It is awkward, difficult, and sometimes humbling, but by persisting in the philosophy that no person can be simply dismissed, a mood is shaped in the classroom that allows for sharing and dialogue.

To suggest that the process of encouraging free expression is simple or painless is mistaken. In many instances, a battle is taking place. Steadfast biases are being challenged by the authors, through class discussions, and yes, by the biases of the teacher. In some cases, I make a student who has been dismissive and superficially critical of an author rewrite a paper, insisting that she/he present the author's view of the topic(s) raised before presenting her/his own. For example, when one student wrote of Leslie Feinberg's *Stone Butch Blues* that it was tragic that Jess couldn't accept her God-given gender and so brought tremendous suffering on herself, I contained the rage that arose from my own resentment of this perspective and suggested that she present *Jess*'s view on the matter before stating her own. At first it felt like a frustrating setback. I felt a responsibility to recognize the student's own right to expression, but I felt an equal responsibility to challenge that view. She claimed, however, that the assignment had opened her mind on this issue.

I have found it quite shocking at times to be confronted with open criticism of gay/lesbian lifestyles. I must be somewhat straight-looking. I have sometimes had to respond to hate-filled comments aimed at gays and lesbians in the classroom, but in this particular case I was also aware that the transgendered character of Leslie Feinberg's novel pushed levels of discomfort for students who felt that they had a grasp on normalcy. Her book, more than any other covered that semester, raised some students' hackles over the idea of accepting diversity, but it also illustrated the transcendent quality of some people's ability to understand and resonate with various positions. One student from Korea expressed the paradoxical view that she had been raised to condemn homosexuality (and by implication, transgendered existence—no matter how many times I sorted out the distinction, the issues were conflated), but felt a particular empathy for Jess, because she too understood the sense of isolation this character felt. In her own particular way, she was affected by this novel.

When racist/classist/genderist remarks have arisen, I have done my best to point out their presence and to offer reasons and examples for my own view. Taking my cue from Howard Zinn, I make it clear to my class that I have a political stance and that I don't hide it or pretend neutrality. From an article entitled "How Free is Public Education?" in the *Zinn Reader*, the following sentiments offer a wonderful guiding philosophy:

> In my teaching I never concealed my political views: my detestation of war and militarism, my anger at racial inequality, my belief in a democratic socialism, in a rational and just distribution of the world's wealth. To pretend to an "objectivity" that was neither possible nor desirable seemed to me dishonest.
>
> I made it clear to my students at the start of each course that they would be getting *my* point of view on the subjects under discussion, that I would try to be fair to other points of view, that I would scrupulously uphold their right to disagree with me.

> My students had a long experience of political indoctrination before they arrived in my class—in family, in high school, in movies and television. They would hear viewpoints other than mine in other courses, and for the rest of their lives. I insisted on my right to enter my opinions in the marketplace of ideas, so long dominated by orthodoxy.[8]

With Howard Zinn's words in mind, I grow more comfortable with saying that teaching in a classroom that emphasizes personal voice sometimes means entering a battlefield. It means entering the classroom as a human being who can be challenged, who has vulnerabilities and limitations, rather than as an all-knowing, impartial judge. It often means sifting through opinions again and again. It often means arguing. It often means hearing things I would rather gloss over and responding not with hatred, but with the courage to confront ideologies that denigrate humanity. In order to find a ground of human connection in the classroom community, the underlying roots of racism, homophobia, genderism, and classism have to be painfully sifted through, and because no class is neutral and no person is neutral, even the philosophy of hatred that calls on seemingly "natural" categories of privilege, power, and prominence must again and again be unraveled.

The challenge, it seems, is to allow for the fact that one is not always in control of a class in which personal voice is encouraged. Patience is called for, as is tolerance, but also one has to do away with fear of confrontation. Every group dynamic is distinct, and every session is open to new possibilities. I may direct discussions or raise particular questions, but I also allow room for students to express their own concerns and interests. In *Teaching to Transgress*, bell hooks writes:

> To begin, the professor must genuinely *value* everyone's presence. There must be an ongoing recognition that everyone influences the classroom dynamic, that everyone contributes. These contributions are resources. Used constructively, they enhance the capacity of any class to create an open learning community.[9]

For myself, the classroom is a dynamic center of interaction between the words of the authors I choose for the reading list, the thoughts and experiences of the students in the class, and my own position as facilitator, reluctant judge, political proselytizer, and harsh critic—someone outspoken enough about my own views that students feel free to be open about their own. I am not a neutral teacher, I don't teach neutral authors, and I don't expect my students to be neutral. This is what allows a space for meaningful self-expression to happen. Fostering a space of freedom in the classroom may sound at first like an easy endeavor, but in fact creating such a space in an institutional setting that reflects the biases and hierarchies of dominant culture is an ongoing struggle and a revolutionary act.

CHAPTER 7

Reflections on Alternative Identities in Contemporary Feminism

S&M

For many young women today, the central practice of feminism is a celebration of radicalism on a personal level rather than a strictly political level. Acts of defiance are celebrated as acts of personal fulfillment meant to inspire others to claim their own ground of self-determination. In defiance of social ordinances and attitudes that suppress the free expression of identity, many women have resorted to the creation of an alternate reality, an alternate space in which they can claim a ground of meaning and expression as irrefutably theirs.

In terms of gender identity, the need for an alternative community space is evident from the political realities of public and legislative hostilities toward gay, lesbian, and transgendered individuals. Female sensuality can be celebrated in a space free of a condescending or humiliating gaze. The resulting empowerment eroticizes women's lives, perhaps in the sense Audre Lorde suggests in "Uses of the Erotic," in which the erotic is seen as the surging forth of the life energy, passion, and joyful vitality that has long been suppressed in women. Lorde explicitly condemned pornography in this essay as a practice that deadens women's enjoyment of their own sensuality by making them fearful of being seen as physical objects to be violently used. But one might argue that even the cheap and tawdry sex of popular lesbian S&M and butch/femme images is meant to reclaim the territory of the body in terms of physical sensuality stolen from women, and that this act is very much in the spirit of Audre Lorde's insightful essay and entreaty.

The idea of sexual freedom is one often associated with gay, lesbian, and transgendered individuals because homosexuality is automatically read by many people as a purely sexual category of identification. By a twisted tautology any homosexual or trans person is read one-dimensionally as solely sexual. They are seen as breaking the rules, thus freely expressing desires and emotions of individuals outside the "law." The assumption is that when puritanical constructs are cast aside, endless possibilities open. Homosexuality, like sexual expression, is read as the place where boundaries and prohibitions are laid aside. The sense of freedom inscribed on homosexuality is shared by certain communities of artists, writers, and other nonconformists in ways that connect sexual freedoms to other psychological, emotional, and spiritual potentials. One can be annoyed at the obvious reductiveness of this association, but it is also possible to celebrate the doorway opened to an escape from mundane, ordinary, and confining beliefs.

When one does not look too closely, it is easy to valorize a lifestyle assumed by champions of liberty, independence, and free speech for women. For example, Pat Califia's theoretical writings on lesbian S&M sex seem to present it as an opening for a spiritual breakthrough by which women can regain control of their sensuality and realize the awesome power of visualization to enhance their sense of themselves. That women's sense of openness and self-affirmation and feelings of sensual power can be shut down by the context of male-induced violence and domination and the relegation of women to the fringes is, I believe, quite evident. But according to Pat Califia and other advocates of S&M sex, the avoidance of controversial images at all costs has created a faded and stagnant form of feminism. In her own critique of her collection of erotic short stories entitled *Melting Point*, she states "If we clean up queer fiction so that it contains nothing that will offend straight people or bolster a negative view of our community, we will wind up with books that are about as satisfying to read as cardboard—a biodegradable literature."[1]

The attitude expressed in this quote serves to silence lesbians who have traditionally woman-affirming feminist ideals—those who advocate that women find new ways to define themselves and their sexuality that transcend the readings of womanhood through a patriarchal gaze. She allows no room for criticism of S&M practices because she claims that such criticism would confine her personal freedom of self-expression. This is true even though as an S&M practitioner she resides in the haven of the gay/lesbian/trans political community because it allows space for freedom and sexual disinhibition. Freedom of identity and freedom of activity are closely aligned, and she, in defending her lifestyle, aligns them with the rights of gender expression upheld by queer activists. As logical and appropriate as this association may be, the corollary she suggests does not really hold true. If the gay rights movement makes room for the S&M freedom movement, it does not follow that it encompasses this movement or must of necessity embrace it. Only a larger movement, one advocating freedom of all sexual expression, would necessarily advocate her views.

The gay rights movement is becoming more and more consciously associated with a broader movement toward acceptance of all gender and sexual expressions, so there is certainly room to speak of a common ground of identification with a woman whose writing is both lesbian and purposely pornographic. But to assume that a reader critical of the S&M content of her fiction is being anti-gay, anti-lesbian, and so on is unjustified and misleading. She writes, "One of the healing functions of gay and lesbian writing is that it confirms our reality and worth as a people. It documents the awful things that oppression has done to us, and it also details the ways we cooperate with that oppression, as well as our struggle for equality and freedom."[2] Given the content of the book in which her reflection is included, it is self-evident that she is speaking of the rights of the S&M community when she affirms gay and lesbian writing. She never distinguishes between these communities, nor does she specifically address the S&M content of her writing in this passage. Granted, these identities may be inextricably blended for her, but that is not true for everyone. For many women, affirmation of their lesbian identity has no conceivable connection to something as far beyond their experience as the contents of Pat Califia's S&M–flavored fiction. Her blending of these two identities serves to silence potential critics and grants her dominance over the territory of lesbian and gay rights because she places herself in the position of defining the aims and boundaries of the gay rights movement. Although she is justified in speaking out for her position and for the "sex-positive" camp (as if anyone who disagrees with her is therefore "sex negative"), my support for her views stops short of blanket acceptance or agreeing not to disagree. A moratorium on criticism of sexually violent and perverse images would strike an unwarranted blow against the efforts of many feminist and lesbian activists.

The women's movement, like the gay rights movement, has been stretched in recent years to accommodate issues of freedom of sexual expression, and debates over pornography versus free expression remain unresolved within the academic community. A 1999 issue of *Hypatia: A Journal of Feminist Philosophy* contained two articles addressing pornographic (and S&M) expression as a feminist issue. In an article entitled "On Pornography, Representation and Sexual Agency," Consuelo Concepcion argues against anti-pornography legislation, claiming that it "could close off any and all dialogue that might give women a much needed sexual language with which to communicate our ideas, desires and practices." She feels that pornography has varying intents, which may in some cases be misogynist but which may also, when created by and for a lesbian S&M audience, affirm women's "differing sexual practices." She adds that "universalization denies women sexual agency because it assumes that our ideas about sexuality have no legitimacy and would be co-opted by the patriarchy."[3] She advocates for the rights of women to represent themselves through sexual agency, but she ignores the fact that women's bodies and even their rights to self-identification have already been co-opted by the patriarchy. The definition of woman, likewise, is steeped in a cultural milieu in which womanhood itself is practically defined as a state in which the individual is objectified by outer forces and, specifically, denied the right of agency. Given this dismal state of affairs, can volitional engagement in pornographic and S&M scenes and public actions ever provide a ground in which self-determination can be enacted? In my opinion, yes. Women who reinvent themselves are always revolutionary. And yet, one cannot deny the stranglehold culture has over the individual in confining and interpreting acts of free expression, even those that are rebellious.

I find myself advocating Consuelo Concepcion's position with the uncomfortable, nagging reservation that I have no desire in doing so to gloss over the existence of many intentionally negative, misogynist, and derogatory representations of women as demeaned others, as denigrated outsiders to be abused and used. Nor do I wish to belittle the effects of such images on the self-image of women as undervalued, lesser citizens. In stating this, I do not feel I am being anti sex, nor am I advocating a shutting down of female and lesbian public expression, and I resent the implication that being a critical thinker makes me an enemy of the "girls just want to have fun" philosophical camp.

In defending the legitimacy of pornography, Concepcion further claims that it "provides many women pleasure and profit."[4] She is unwilling to examine the negative aspects of coercion and self-hatred that may also be at work. She also overlooks the desperation and hopelessness of poverty, as if every woman has an array of career choices and opportunities open to her of which participating in the production and sale of pornographic images of her body is just one. However, as in the case of prostitution, I think it is possible to advocate the rights of free choice of the individuals involved and still critically question exploitative practices used against women and other sexually vulnerable individuals. For example, within the American context, it may be possible to argue for the rights of women to choose prostitution as a legitimate profession. In the Philippines, however, where I lived for two years as a Peace Corps volunteer, and in Thailand, I met and spoke with several female and male prostitutes and developed a sense of the larger milieu in which these individuals existed. The general image I carried away was not one of free choice.

In both of these countries, prostitution often entailed enslavement to a club or individual. Runaways could be returned by the police to their owners because they were property. It was not uncommon for children to be sent by parents, who sacrificed them with the expectation that money would be sent home and that the "shamed one" would never again show her/his face in the home community. At Subic Bay Naval base in the Philippines, which was still in operation during my term of Peace Corps service, soldiers walked around the base with young women on their arms, and the streets outside the base were lined with what seemed like hundreds of brothels and prostitute bars. It was reported to me that the highest prices went for virgins and that there was stiff competition for the youngest girl available, who was often only twelve or thirteen years old.

One woman I knew, a Buddhist whose father had been a civil rights lawyer "gotten rid of" by the Marcos regime, had a young girl living in her small apartment. She told me at first that she was her maid. I was naively puzzled by this statement, because the 11-year-old seemed more interested in watching cartoons on TV than cleaning, and it did not seem like my ethical friend to live off child labor. She later confided that the girl had been sent by her parents to Manila with a one-way boat ticket. I still did not understand. "To be a prostitute. What else would she do to survive?" my friend finally said. She and other civic-minded women were trying to organize a home and refuge for children deserted to prostitution, but in the meantime, she had given this girl a home.

I met other women, some barely teenagers, who spoke to me of dreams of meeting rich Americanos who would take them home to the land of plenty to be their wives. They spoke of the lack of opportunity in their villages. The racism of systems in which Asian prostitutes are offered up to American military men, western tourists, Japanese businessmen, and others was appallingly evident. In discussions with a woman who was organizing an advocacy group for prostitutes, I learned that there were few avenues for these women to turn to, which meant that they were prey to rapists, pedophiles, and abusers, as long as the client had enough money. I also remember a discussion I had with a young Manila socialite on a ferry. She was well dressed and well educated. We were both aware of the young women prostitutes accompanying mostly aging and decrepit drunken foreigners on the deck near us on their way to an island vacation resort. I was watching one young woman alternately smile and then frown and glare every time the man with the wallet looked away. Her eyes were hauntingly empty and devoid of hope. The woman next to me shrugged in the midst of our brief conversation and said simply, "You can't blame them. Everybody has their price."

I am not alone in my reaction to Concepcion's stance in favor of pornography as free expression. The second article contributed to *Hypatia* on the issue of feminism and pornography presents a more critical view of the potential for exploitation while still advocating individual freedoms. It is entitled, "Pornography's Many Meanings: A Reply to C.M. Concepcion", and its author, Alisa Carse, while viewing pornography as harmful, nonetheless states that "the struggle against pornography must be waged through educatic expressive exploration, and protest, not through the law."[5] Her reasoning is that such laws would indeed inhibit expression of and discourse about non-harmful sexual activities. She claims instead to advocate "respect for the realities of sexual difference and the multiplicity of interpretations and meanings given to texts and images."[6] Her point resonates for me in the warnings that were posted on television prior to screenings of the *Ellen* show, once Ellen Degeneres, the show's star, had come out as a lesbian onscreen and off. Her show, by this warning, was deemed explicit and pornographic, shocking and unfit for the gaze of easily influenced teenagers and youngsters. The term lesbian was conflated with the notion of uninhibited female sexuality and inflammatory images of unleashed desire—women out of control. In this sense, Pat Califia's blending of the causes of gay freedom and sexual freedom seems justified.

Alisa Carse defines pornography narrowly, in order to distinguish it from the arena of free and consensual sexual expression, as that which takes "moral harm (or specifically the subordination of women) to be constitutive of pornography's meaning."[7] Blanket acceptance of sexual expression, whether in body or image, leaves no basis whatsoever for criticism of any expression, regardless of whether it is an original, experimental, "artistic" image or the ingrained, unconscious repetition of a damaging and perverse stereotype that may be obviously misogynist and may contain racist overtones as well.

The difficulty Alisa Carse faces is that judgments of distasteful and aberrant images are always subject to individual perspective.

And in fact, she refines her view from an earlier position by claiming that the context as well as the content must be considered.[8] How does one tell what the intent of a piece is or who the audience is?

Even though Carse allows that there is no way to police images and in fact feels that regulating laws is impractical, she insists on the need to pass judgment. However, the line she draws between the offensive and the experimental (that which is created solely to produce an effect) is unclear unless one is willing to place oneself in the role of moral judge. Even then, the outcome may be far from clear, as in the case of the writings of Pat Califia, who creates unfathomably outrageous and sadistic images to stir things up in order to release hidden desires in her readers' imaginations and confound their beliefs about what is right, what is okay, and what is clearly wrong. Pat Califia seems intent on reclaiming the term pornography and cleansing it from negative connotations, in much the same way that the term "queer" has been reclaimed as an umbrella term by gay, lesbian, bi, and trans activists. However, like Alisa Carse, I have to ask where tolerance stops, and I want to know the location of that limit and to be sure that a limit exists. In a sense, I read Carse's position as advocating discussion. She wants to remind us that many of us are uncomfortable with certain images and that as women, we are all too accustomed to having our limits violated, often against our will. I agree that we shouldn't let this matter rest by glibly endorsing any and all sexually explicit images.

It is difficult, however, at least from a creative point of view, to demarcate a limit, and moreover, to justify an argument against the right to freedom of expression. Pat Califia's writing is groundbreaking, and even if it isn't everyone's cup of tea, its unabashed existence has had a tremendous impact on the acceptance of S&M in feminist and lesbian communities by its focus on individual prerogative. I can't say I personally find in her approach grounds for affirmation or respect for women's identity. At the same time, I wish I could say I found it easy to put down her stories once I started turning the pages. But of course, every viewer of popular horror and action films might easily find her/himself in the position of being horrified and mesmerized at the same time. Powerful, evocative images claim us and affect us, and yet, shouldn't we stop looking if it offends us? And if we don't stop looking, who should we blame?

I claim the right to disagree with offensive images. I will not stand silently by if I feel disgusted or threatened. I feel no obligation to accept every practice and viewpoint. In disagreeing, I do not silence anyone but instead express my view freely. In fact, if a story related to me by a writer I met at a conference is accurate, even Califia's defense of artistic freedom has its limits. Apparently, acting on a board of editors, Pat Califia objected to the use of a gun used in a story to threaten a woman. The writer I met was irritated by this event and exclaimed, "After what she's written, she's going to censor me?" My point is that we all have the right to express our opinions and as intelligent beings we should express them, but just as Pat Califia is not obligated to endorse every S&M image in fictional writings, other lesbians and feminists are not obligated to accept without criticism images they find degrading or violent toward women.

I am interested, however, in Pat Califia's emphasis on creative visualization as the focus of sensual and personal encounters because I see visualization as a transformative force. For women reclaiming the right to create their reality, fantasy is a powerful tool. From a theoretical standpoint, Califia's affirmation of the transformative power of erotic energy resonates with Audre Lorde's affirmation of the uses of erotic power. I am fascinated by the possibility of being more present in one's life by reclaiming it psychologically and physically, particularly in cases where social forces have been specifically aimed at inhibiting the sense of presence, and the right to be present, in women and other marginalized figures. However, I am leery of grungy realities, and I am hesitant to critically examine S&M fiction, because I think it might hurt the case of an all-accepting embrace of S&M sex as empowering to women. Read on the surface, it is debasing to the individuals involved, and debasing, by association, to women. And yet the real question is what the individuals involved are feeling, and that is a question that only those individuals can answer.

The position I wind up endorsing is that S&M has the potential, at least theoretically, to open doors for women, because it enlivens the rebel-hero image of women as powerful possessors of dangerous forces to be reckoned with. S&M practices also heighten the image of women as sexual and sensual. And it may exist among lesbians without the fear that objectification and violence create among women, although that point is debatable. Several women I have spoken to have expressed to me that S&M "play," including role-playing, has opened up avenues of sensual experience that were severely cut off for them and has helped to heal old emotional scars. At a workshop at a conference, a group of young women, many of whom were under twenty-one and in their teens, were the most vocal adherents of the idea that sensual freedom is linked to freedom of gender expression and freedom of identity in general. They affirmed the right to create, recreate, and alter, time and again, their own sense of identity and their right to be the ones to control their bodies and expression of sensuality. Because they too seemed to see S&M in the light that I have just expressed, I felt even more justified in my assumption that many contemporary feminists who champion individual freedom above all else embrace S&M, at least theoretically, as sex positive and empowering to women.

However, not everyone is a theorist, and not everyone is reaching for a higher ground to support their actions. For some, S&M is probably no more deeply thought about than the release of violent sexual energy, and although it may be transforming, that transformation is not necessarily positive. It could simply be an expression of despair and anger, of misogyny, and of other base, violent impulses that a person gives over to unconsciously. In fact, viewed on the surface, there is not much to say about exploitation and gratification through pain, except that it is sad that we have been so conditioned by a controlled and exploitive, dehumanizing society that we are numb and feel neither our own pain nor the pain of others. The underlying possibility for the value of S&M hinges on the power to dream and create for oneself fantasy worlds that provide release from a flat, dismal, and unerotic social context and individual reality. It is this potential that I am interested in, because I see it as an avenue of transformation strongly embraced by the contemporary feminist movement, perhaps partly due to spiritual philosophies that advocate personal empowerment, such as yoga, meditation, and visualization.

Butch and Femme

It seems that butch (and sometimes, occasionally, femme) and f-t-m transgender figures currently hold sway as paragons of lesbian feminist freedom and sexual icons. Photographs of butch women and articles on butch styles fill "progressive" lesbian magazines such as *Girlfriends*. Seen as vanguards of women's freedom to choose and create identity and sensuality and, in a sense, as channels bursting through the dams of gender conformity that hold women back, literary figures such as the character Jesse from Leslie Feinberg's *Stone Butch Blues* are valorized as protectors and lovers of women. From a comfortable distance, this is seen as affirmative and progressive, rather than as a regression to polarized, specifically delineated gender roles that conform to patterns of the 1950s. In practice, as a movement, advocates for butch/femme expression stumble over the disparity between these two distinct readings. The promise of gender freedom is strictly countered by a policing, on a group and individual level, of gender representation. Several women I know who are in butch/femme relationships have felt policed into behaving in a feminine manner, which all too often has meant dressing to conform to a feminine ideal and acting with an exaggerated pretense of helplessness, passivity, and so on. For those for whom it works, great. There are many possible scenarios in which femininity is empowering and butch identity is masculine without being overbearing. In other words, for those for whom either identity actually seems to match personal identity, great, but for many others, especially those who seek a clear sense of identity through the simplicity of social conformity, embracing such identities may be a path to closing down rather than opening up a range of possible gender expression. Nonetheless, gender freedom in the form of butch gender expression is currently iconized and valorized as being on the forefront of a movement of self-actualization and self-affirmation for women. This is possibly also true for femme gender expression, though less prominence seems granted femme identity in public forums such as anthologies, conferences, and online chat groups, except as an adjunct to butch identity, which is inevitably granted center stage.

For many people, butch identity represents the paragon of feminist liberation—a woman unconstrained by her gender. Butch identity is seen as a site of individual choice, independent thought, strength of will, and determination—as masculine ground reclaimed by women brave and brazen enough to bulldoze their way onto territory formerly denied women. For example, Rose Tremain's novel *Sacred Country* affirms butch(f-t-m) identity as a paragon of freedom and self-determination. The novel's central figure, Mary, later known as Martin, is one of the few figures in the cast of characters to find a sense of fulfillment by freeing herself from a quagmire of expectations and obligations regarding social identity when she disappears from her childhood community and reappears as Martin, a man virtually unhindered by the past.

An underlying feminist motivation for Martin's escape from female gender is evident in the images Tremain presents of the shackles female identity represent for young Mary/Martin as she/he grows up in an utterly sexist home and community environment. Feminist justifications for Martin's transformation are presented in abundance, suggesting that we, as feminist readers, have a strong stake in the success of Martin's experiment. The fact that his lifespan carries him through the feminist revolutions of the 1960s also indicates that his physical transformation is meant to be read as a culminating image of feminist ideals. Mary/Martin chooses to be an outsider to her/his culture, because that culture has already rejected her/him. She has no hope if she chooses to live her life as a woman in that culture. Hence, she/he is presented not only as a transgender success story but also as a kind of feminist success story. In reflections that reinforce his decision to affirm a psychological gender transformation, he despairs in his pathetic situation as a woman:

> And then I remembered something awful: in the whole of the Dictionary of Inventions, which spanned nine centuries, there was only one woman inventor. Only one! Even the wool-combining machine and the stocking frame had been invented by men. It made me feel terrible, sad as the wind.[9]

The hopelessness felt by young Mary/Martin is exacerbated by the setting at the beginning of the novel of a small English town facing the challenges of growing poverty and a sense of becoming obsolete in modern times. The threat to Mary's survival is not imminent but is instead the possibility of succumbing to the apathy that eats away at the borders of identity for each person in her life and in the decaying village as a whole. The general overtone of the novel is grim, hopeless, and starkly unembellished. Each character's life, as viewed from the inside, is a gray and tattered version of the wishes and dreams they hold dear. In most cases, a split emerges between the dreams that dance on the horizon and the violent self-denial and self-recrimination that make up the contours of their ordinary lives, whose uncrossable boundaries are fenced in with fear and dread of the unknown. Over the decades the small farms of the countryside give way to chicken factories and mechanized farming, converting many farmers into broken, unemployed men. Mary's father, an angry alcoholic, is one of this group. He is abominable and pitiful. His farm is falling into disarray as small farming becomes increasingly obsolete as a viable occupation. Economic oppression and institutional devaluation of the individual tear his sense of dignity to shreds, and he takes out his angst on his unruly daughter, as if she is the one domain of which he may still be master. He is mean-spirited toward Mary. He kills her pet bird Marguerite after it attacks her brother Tim. She responds silently:

> I didn't dare think about Margarite, her veined legs, her speckled sides. I put her into the past. Some of the past is visible and some of it isn't and I hoped the bit of it with Marguerite would stay hidden. But I had this thought about suffering: I thought, I will suffer a lot, I will grow a man's skin. If I suffer and refuse to cry, a penis will grow out of all that is locked away inside. It needs only time.[10]

Her father treats her as alien and worthless, partly because of her femaleness but also because he is threatened by her audacity and masculine affectations. She counters his callous indifference and occasionally violent attitude with a desire to create her own ground of being, the all-important phallus, the signature of significance.

Mary's father is emotionally estranged from his wife, Mary's mother, who is emotionally ill. He expects her to perform as a wife and mother, cooking and cleaning without complaint, and he has no idea how to offset the vacuity of their lives, which she escapes with her illness. Her mother, Marty's rejected role model, sees herself as a hollow onion; no matter how many layers peel away from her, there is never a core. She is harassed and isolated; she fills her days in and out of the hospital with television and airy visions. In moments of clarity, she sees her life as faded and miserable. She feels for Mary occasionally and knows that she is wronged by her abusive father. However, she does not defend her. She embodies the failure and irrelevance of womanhood. She is the doomed, object-like identity awaiting Mary if she cannot escape into a life with depth and meaning—that of a man.

The manhood Mary seeks is not the disillusioned and crumbling figure of manhood her father represents. His masculinity, pressured by faltering economic circumstances, is threatened, for masculinity is a social position of status. Perhaps she wishes to resurrect it or to free it from its impoverishment and humiliation. As her father rages against helplessness, she is often the hapless target of his frustration. But she rages beside him as well as against him, as if she is striving to free him as well as herself. The masculine identity she creates is heroic and necessarily removed from her immediate environment; her masculine image of herself is a literal embodiment of freedom from her dismal circumstances. But it is also as if she is taking over where others have failed.

As she destroys the woman in herself, Mary/Marty dismantles the association she/he shares with her/his mother. Although her attitude toward her mother is affectionate and her murderous rage is reserved for her ineffectually masculine brother, Timmy, Mary/Marty's transition to manhood entails more than attaining masculinity and assuming the stature culturally allotted to masculine existence. It also necessitates an eradication of the feminine, which in this case is embodied in Mary's mother, a woman who has self-imploded in her own despair. She is outwardly inexpressive, embarrassingly meek and docile. Her angst and anguish are never allowed expression.

If there is one source of emotion never unearthed by the courageous Mary/Marty, willing to undergo the task of self-discovery and self-creation into manhood, it is the rage she/he feels toward her/his acquiescing mother. Mary, the child, is responding to an impulse toward freedom when she declares herself Martin, which implies a need to escape an unsatisfactory sense of herself as a woman. Tremain seems to suggest that Mary views female identity as a diseased state. Marty rages because there is no escape. But she has a way out—the secret that she's really a boy.

Tremain shapes the novel to highlight the emotional underpinnings of Mary's decision to become Martin; she thus shapes the transition with a feminist cast. In becoming a man, Mary becomes a liberated woman in that she gains the only freedom apparently open to women in a cultural context dominated by men. It is as if she emerges out of the shadows and into being in her transition to manhood. Manhood, for her, is equivalent with selfhood, autonomy, and the ability to shape destiny. And in these qualities she excels and cuts a finer figure of a "man" than many of her male acquaintances.

For example, Timmy, Mary's brother, seems unassertive, as if his presence is an inexplicable accident of fate with which he has nothing to do. He disengages from emotional and physical neglect into a world of anonymous swimming matches, then seminary; eventually he escapes his looming "imprisonment on the family farm" and ventures off into the happily-ever-after life of marriage to Pearl, a feminine and equally unassertive young lady, who also happens to be the lifelong object of Marty's veneration and infatuation.[11] To Mary, he is an unwitting rival first for her father's love and later for Pearl's.[12] And worse, he doesn't seem to appreciate his "accidental" masculinity. He takes his status and his father's adoration and hope for granted.

As deep-seated as her masculine identity seems to be, perhaps even biologically grounded for all anyone can say, the author leaves ample room for, and in fact paves the way toward, a psychological and feminist analysis of Mary's situation. She is angry with her brother, the apple of her father's eye. It is impossible to overlook one particularly tense chapter that threatens to take a grisly turn when she is practicing magic in order to impress a girl at school she has fallen for. She is perhaps ten at the time and has already taken to calling herself Marty. She has already mastered several tricks but decides to learn the old standby of thrusting swords into a wooden box, which contains none other than her little brother. She sharpens lawn-mower blades into swords and practices with her brother before the grand performance, letting slip to the reader the ominous revelation that her brother will have to hold very still indeed to avoid injury. At the last moment, her father discovers the apparently unconscious plot and saves his son, but the unsettling awareness of her near-success, or perhaps unintentional failure, is not easily dismissed.

There are hints of abuse; Mary's father kills her pet pheasant after it attacks her brother, and he rips away the bandages that hide her teenage breasts. The abuse described suggests borderline sexual trauma. She is also jealous of her father, who wields all the power in the household, even if he is a pitiful, weak and violent character:

> Sonny cut into the wad of bandage in the cleft between Mary's breasts .... She could smell his body which had never touched hers since she was a little girl in his arms. She felt a sickly sorrow, like a dose of poison going into her and spreading all through her.
>
> She started to cry. This was the thing she never wanted to do and never wanted him to see as long as she lived. Not crying was what had given her hope. Now she was sobbing and she couldn't stop. She begged him to let go of her. Screamed and begged.[13]

It is not surprising that Marty runs away after the bandage incident. She reaches adulthood in a former teacher's house and later in London, where she dresses as a man. Although her life there is not rosy, she survives, which is more than can be said for the other inhabitants of this sad story, for she survives not only physically but also in spirit. She has the weight of her own will, daring, endurance and imagination to fall back on. She has her own created reality and so doesn't have to settle for whatever circumstances may bring her.

I suspect that all too many women remember childhood feelings of anger and jealousy over the privileged status of masculinity. I once asked a mostly female freshman/sophomore class if anyone was a feminist. A sprinkling of hands were raised, and most of the others expressed the usual reticence about being viewed as a whiny "bitch" who hates men, as an "unnatural" woman unable to accept the status quo. They led me to believe that they couldn't really think of any specific issues and that I was dragging them into uncomfortable territory by even bringing it up. Then, just as the discussion seemed to be going nowhere, on a sudden impulse I asked about brothers, specifically if women had been treated differently by their parents than their brothers. The room exploded in clamor and the rest of the period was taken up by countless examples of double standards and expectations. I could barely get a word in edgewise. Everywhere there was resentment of their brothers' freedom of movement and freedom from domestic chores and resentment that they were expected to follow in their mothers' footsteps in terms of serving others and acquiescing to other people's demands.

In another class that had several male students mixed in with a female majority, I asked if anyone crossed gender expectations as kids. All the women had some examples to share, and about a third proudly, almost defiantly, declared that they had been tomboys who liked to climb trees and so on, although now of course they liked to wear dresses and so on. For some reason it was important to point this out to everyone—perhaps because the gender-bending grace period for girls had run out by age eighteen or so. Of the men in the class, only one could, or was willing publicly to, recall any incident that crossed genders. He was a young man who stated simply that his mother had influenced him to be gentle and thoughtful, traits apparently not seen as masculine in the cultural mix of their generation. The members of the class who had been influenced by feminism saw nothing unusual in women transgressing into male territory. In fact, they saw it as laudable and progressive as long as a claim to feminine identity was maintained. In other words, as long as the category of the feminine was being stretched, nobody sensed anything unusual. The men, on the other hand, seemed to express no desire to inhabit the traditional world of women in terms of appearance or activity, suggesting that it would be shameful, or perhaps simply that nothing was to be gained by it.

Mary's envy of masculine identity seems to focus primarily on the importance it has in her culture. When Lindsey, the girl Marty secretly loves as a teenager, talks about her new, and first, love experience with a young man and the excitement she feels in submission, erasure, and sublimation to his godlike presence, her comments reinforce Mary's sense of her insignificance as a woman and foster a desire to usurp his throne:

> She said: "I never knew about *giving* myself before, Mary. About, you know, absolutely *submitting*. But this is what's so fantastic about it. I mean, to have Ranulf on top of me and making me do whatever he wants...and I want to, that's the thing, I mean, do whatever he wants, not what I want and when he comes—you know about coming, don't you?—he always tells me, he says God I'm coming Lindsey, I'm coming and I think God he's coming and I feel so...*privileged*."[14]

In private fantasies, Mary responds by replacing herself as the one who responds to Lindsey's adoration:

> I had been a chaste person. Now, at night, in my coffin bed, I become Martin Ward, Lindsey's lover. I couldn't help it. She should not have told me what Ranulf did to her. She made me want it. I laid her underneath me. My breasts became hers. I closed my eyes. She begged me to go deeper into her, to hurt her. She said, "Destroy me, Martin." And when I finished, she was bruised, she was crying. I licked her tears. I whispered to the wet pillow: "Lindsey, it's your own fault."[15]

Her stated desire to explore Lindsey, to obliterate her with her awesome presence and fill her with a greater force could also be read as a desire to destroy the feminine within herself. Although her fantasies with Lindsey are not fulfilled, she asserts her own existence through them and apparently solidifies her sense of manhood. The successful characters in Tremain's novel, which include Marty, settle for survival as long as they can have some freedom of movement and a place of refuge where they won't be disturbed. They are better off than the sad characters who accept their miserable fates and suffer the slow burn of monotony where life should be, but even they do not have the luxury of absolute fulfillment.

Recognizing the valor and integrity of the outsider, of the oppressed, of those who are heroic and defiant simply by surviving is a central theme of the novel which resonates, sometimes painfully. Blindness to privilege is one way of living unaware. As in gender discrimination, racial discrimination is overtly present for those who suffer from it. They have no choice but to be aware, and their awareness places them a step above the unimaginative oppressors.

In a sense, Mary has a greater hope of freedom than the others in the novel because she is aware that her fetters exist and knows that her survival hinges on her ability to fight her way into a better life. She must take up the task of actively becoming the creator of her own life; she has been exiled from society before she could even enter it. What is at stake is more than gender, more than identity. What is at stake is the possibility of freedom and intelligence:

> I remembered it now and it helped me to see something else. My own literal answer to the debate entitled "Who am I?" was: "Martin Ward. A boy." The set answer, the one that everybody knew and expected was: "Mary Ward. A girl." I had never ever in sixteen years dared to give the literal answer because I was afraid to be loathed.... To be hated by my

> father was enough for me. I was too cowardly to risk being hated by the whole world and to hear only silence falling around me and then a voice of authority telling me to sit down.[16]

As Marty's adult life unfolds, his process of coming into his own identity is paralleled with the story of Walter, a man from her/his village who rejects family tradition by refusing to follow in his father's footsteps. He rejects the family butcher business. He is also gay, or at least has a relationship with a man, which emboldens him to change his life by moving to London and later to the United States to pursue a career as a country singer. He is someone whose life is similar to Mary's in that he has the courage to come up with a dream and follow it. His gay relationship represents the starting point of his move toward setting out on his own in uncharted territory. The relationship coincides with the cessation of disturbing dreams he has of a grandfather who coerces him into maintaining the family business and who, until he disappears altogether, appears in increasingly lewd images. The dream figure represents the repressive force of authority holding back erotic energy and life energy. Walter's freedom is closely linked in nature to Mary's, who finds in her gender and sexual freedom a pervasive freeing of her spirit and energy, which makes a happy, if not perfect, life possible for her.

This novel establishes a clear connection between the freeing of sexual energy from the confines of "permissible" love that lacks originality and the ability to live a life with artistic energy and intelligence. In this way sexual issues assume an existential dimension in freeing the individual to truly live by daring to explore beyond entrenched mores.

After a daring move to London, where Mary dresses as a man and dates women, she decides to make the physical transition to manhood. Her first step is to visit a doctor, who scorns her and treats her as a freak. The doctor views Mary's sense of gender identity as a disorder. She is forced to trust in her own reality. She has no support and knows that her views are grossly at odds with the society with which she is forced to coexist.[17]

Marty must create her life path on her own, without guidance or sympathy. When she visits the psychiatrist authorized to approve the surgeries she wishes to undergo, she is called upon to prove that she is a man psychologically. "He asked me whether I could mend an electric fuse and whether I knew the rules of cricket. He said: 'Do you enjoy or repudiate domestic tasks, such as hoovering?' He said: 'Are you jealous of men's superior strength?' He said: 'Have you ever been train spotting?'"[18] He chose what he thought were characteristically male interests to define manhood. The interview was pointless, as his mundane examples of masculinity illustrate. For him, masculinity was nothing more than conforming to cultural expectations and social surroundings.

Enter Pearl, future wife of Marty's brother Tim. She visits Marty, and he adores her. She is perfectly feminine, naive, beautiful, trusting, and innocent. She does not think innovatively about herself or her future, a fact that, unfortunately, seems to make her perfect wife material.

Marty's desire for Pearl suggests a hope that could save her from impending male domination. Pearl is anything but a feminist. She is compliant and is at the mercy of whoever takes the position of director and caretaker of her. And yet it never occurs to Marty to empower her so that she will not lose the core of her being—to a man. Instead, she/he tries to possess her. She/he is focused on taking the position of a man in relation to her rather than in appreciating her as a full human being. She/he wants to guide her, hold her, care for her, and sexually claim her. But Pearl repels Marty's advances and accuses her/him of treating her like an object rather than a person, an action that seems, incongruously enough, to suggest a great deal of emotional insight. When Pearl marries Timmy, Marty struggles to regain a sense of legitimacy as a man. He inherits 1,000 pounds, which gives him an air of self-sufficiency:

> I bought a new suit and a kipper tie. I had my shoes shined. I gave tips to people.
>
> I went into bars and bought drinks for young women and sometimes I put my hand on their silky legs or touched the top of their breasts.[19]

Gender, for Marty, becomes concretely defined by erotic sexual connection. He becomes a man most fully in disguise, in relationships where he is passing as a man and treated as a man. In such cases, outward social cues predominate, such as the air of confidence he acquires once he has money to give tips and buy drinks. What is a man, then? Body or attitude? If it is attitude, it is something more than a gender. It is a position of power and authority over others. It is the capacity to take up space in the world according to social position. When Marty has wealth and a sense of self-ownership, he feels he has earned the "right" to take the sexual initiative and to treat the world as his. His money, as much as his dress and physical gender, is a mark of masculinity more potent than cologne.

That spirit of independence Marty and the other dreamers of the novel express is at the core of the contemporary lesbian feminist movement's focus on the right to self-expression and the power of visualization and fantasy to recreate the individual. Defiance is survival, so those whose very existence is seen as an affront to "natural law" by the general public—that is, those who are transgendered, gay, or lesbian; those who participate in S&M relationships and so forth—are forced to live as outlaws and to pave their own way. In the end, Tremain portrays Mary/Marty as lucky because she had to push the boundaries of the erotic, even though she was forced to do so. Her explorations stirred a whole new being within her, and she was alive in a way that others in the novel were not because they followed the cultural prescriptions about their destinies. Only the exceptional survive, it would seem. Because Mary, from a young age, is exceptional not only in terms of gender identity but in terms of confidence and willingness to shape events rather than allow them to shape her, she is an exceptional human being.

As in the case of Jess in Leslie Feinberg's *Stone Butch Blues*, the challenge makes the person, in the sense that facing the stigma of being an outsider can produce wisdom and integrity. It is commonly supposed that difficulty causes bitterness, that being the object of hatred crushes the spirit. But fear and vulnerability can be an impetus for growth.

In this light, the ability to live outside the ordinary context is empowering. Unearthing oppression in its subtle and gross forms is likewise fulfilling and empowering to oppressed individuals. One of the fears of contemporary feminism is that dwelling on women's oppression is disempowering because it creates a sense of identity based on victimization. But when one sees "victims" as people who understand the need to think for themselves, who trust their inner voices, their hearts, their erotic energy, and their intelligence, the status of victim takes on new meaning. And when one sees oppressors as people whose minds are so contorted with hate that they cannot even think clearly, the question of who is the true victim becomes very real. The oppressors seem to be, from this light, in a zombie-like, non-living, painfully unenergized state, while the oppressed and the ostracized are the creators of their own psychic life, and in fact, their own world. Rather than being the tragic misfit her childhood fantasies and anger might have suggested, Marty the adult is a hero and a cultural icon for the next generation. In the 1950s, the butch was denigrated, but now she is enjoying a renaissance among many lesbians in the contemporary feminist movement. They see in the butch a symbol of power to admire and seek shelter in. Leslie Feinberg was the first to articulate the image of the new butch in her novel *Stone Butch Blues,* of course. In Jess we found a butch we could love, a peaceful figure who was a union organizer and a feminist, a lover who knew how to cherish and honor women.

But *Stone Butch Blues* presents a picture of the butch world that is perhaps too rigid. The butches in Feinberg's novel must ride their Harleys. The warriors are venerated and the enemies are clear. But Jess makes no distinction between the police who rape and sexually humiliate their transgender prisoners and the feminists who are unable to deal with a woman who is a man. Feinberg is harshly critical of such feminists and presents those who are active in the butch/femme scene as the defenders of freedom. The result is that all critical examination of gender expression and regulation is curtailed. For example, how do we define feminism? Is it enough to venerate women? Can that veneration itself be defining and controlling? Jess, after all, loves "high" femmes, not ordinary pants-wearing women.

It seems as if androgyny is the worst sin of all for some members of the butch/femme movement, for all the superficial talk of gender tolerance. Androgynous lesbians do not present themselves clearly and consistently in hyped-up masculine or feminine accouterments, and they are consistently despised by a number of pro-butch/femme theorists as sexless and out of touch with their own potential sensuality. They are seen as lesser beings, not as feminists, not as modern women, but as dangerous, threatening figures who themselves are misguided and lost.

In contrast, those in the butch/femme movement see themselves as women in touch with their gender and sexual identities, women who are not afraid to acknowledge primal forces that move within them. Furthermore, they are presented as free of the limitations of culture, particularly the limitations imposed by earlier feminists who challenged gender identities that limited women to roles as lesser beings. The very women who fought the battles that have given us the freedom of self-expression we enjoy today as women and as lesbians are being tacitly condemned as the reactionary forces that must now be overcome in the enlightened millennium.

For example, in an advice column in *GirlTalk* magazine, Pat Califia responds to a reader's question about the resurgence of butch/femme relationships with a stern lecture. The reader asks, "Why after all these years would anyone want to limit themselves to that kind of role-playing?"

She answers,

> In my not-at-all-humble opinion, butch-femme never went away and is not going through a resurgence now; it has always been a part of lesbian culture. But there was a period during the late 1970's and most of the 1980's when it was political suicide to admit this. Women who identify as butch or femme are not "limiting themselves," they are expressing their deepest desires and making their core identities public. It's not a game of dress-up or let's pretend, although, as you point out, there would be nothing wrong with an evening spent acting out butch-femme roles as a hot sexual fantasy. Butch-femme continues to exist because it is an effective way for some of us to signal our sexual intentions and romantic hopes.
>
> There are more options for lesbians now, but I don't think butch-femme will ever be extinct. In fact, if you sat down right now and made a list of your friends, I bet you would be able to tell me which women are butch and which are femme.[20]

This is not in line with my experience at all. For example, I recall the contortions a group of young graduate student lesbian women I was among went through to define themselves accurately. I could only laugh as, straight-faced and serious, we each tried to find some combination that worked. Butchy femme, soft butch with a femmy side, a femmy-butch femme...fortunately it stopped before it became too absurd. My sense was that no one among us wanted to give up her right to feel like a beautiful sensual woman or give up her claim to power and authority.

When she speaks about lesbian sexuality, Califia obliterates the possibility of individual expression that differs from her own and, in fact, she dictates the terms of lesbian sexuality by demanding center stage for butch/femme relationships and identities. She also assumes that butch/femme expression has only one meaning across the board, ignoring the possibility of individual expression in which role identity is a kind of dressing up and experimentation and, in some cases, fashion. Interest in the butch/femme community has gained momentum, as evidenced by sales and publication of many new books and articles on the subject. And interest in butch/femme style has also proliferated. Whether the fashion of choice is a buzz cut, a sleeveless black T-shirt, motorcycle boots, or a suit, a mood and a message are conveyed.

For Califia, the outer expressions of butch/femme identity correspond to an inner, unalterable core of being. This implies that unified and universal identities exist for every lesbian, which is an outrageous claim. It means that gender identities are in no way unique or subject to individual readings of masculinity and femininity. In fact, in her statement in *Girltalk,* Califia doesn't speak of broad concepts such as masculinity and femininity. Instead, she refers to butch and femme as categories that transcend time and individuality. She ignores the fact that for young women today, these concepts may be based in a nostalgia for the lesbian counterculture of the 1950s and earlier. These romanticized figures of the past have a mystique similar to Hollywood cowboys, of whom stories and fantasies obscure individual acts and daily struggles. In fantasy, images of lesbians past become more present than lesbians of today; they lurk in the shadows in a dreamed world of steamy bars, dark windowless rooms, and speakeasies. These fantasy women are heightened with an edge of criminality in which the defiant rebel overthrows the established order in a glorious and intoxicating rush of emotion. With sexual force, the image promises release.

As fantasy and fashion, these images are powerful because some aspect of identity is created by cultural expression. However, the category "butch" does not encompass masculinity, nor does the category "femme" encompass femininity. This is precisely why butch and femme individuals ran into conflict with feminist ideologies of the 1970s and 1980s designed to redefine possibilities for femininity (and also masculinity). Feminists were actively discarding stereotypes about femininity, and they met with a great deal of resistance in the culture at large. Such women were not interested in replicating a femininity that looked like what the patriarchy wanted them to exhibit.

The very words butch and femme conjure up the 1950s: femme women in fishnet stockings (something I never heard of until butch and femme came into vogue), lipstick, and dressy dresses, and butch women with slicked back hair wearing suits and ties, elegantly polite, holding doors, paying for dinner. Such old-fashioned gallantry is not necessarily antifeminist. However, as times changed, feminists in relationships with other women grew to expect to have old ideas about gender identity challenged.

In contemporary times, even among women I know who consider themselves femme, many draw limits on their marriage to a fixed identity. They see their femininity as a side of themselves sometimes in conflict with their sense of self-sufficiency, freedom, and ambition. Although some women see their femme side as powerful and assert it, others feel that its expression involves submission and a curtailing of personal will. They themselves may hold forth an image of femme they consider to be retrograde and helpless, wholly inadequate to the expression of their whole being yet supremely sexy and desirable. They define femme as a limited category, as something to try on in order to enhance a sense of sensuality and self-love, but not as a full identity.

It is ironic that the butch/femme movement purports to be about individual freedom, but in fact some segments of it have become extremely conservative in their dictation of "proper" gender roles. One year some friends and I attended a conference for f-t-m and butch individuals and their supporters. We all expected to find something groundbreaking going on. We expected to find challenges to gender roles. Instead, we found, with few exceptions, (and those almost exclusively among those involved in S&M and among the very young), reinforcements of the social values and gender roles of the 1950s and 1960s. I distinctly remember one woman, who was dressed impeccably in a suit and looked very handsome, who framed a question to the group about her fears of transitioning by stating that she was most worried about not being able to support her family, implying that the beautifully dressed woman she was with had no role in financial support but was there to be taken care of. This was not the case, but the image conformed to a familiar pattern of gender roles.

On another occasion at the same conference, an f-t-m man who stood out from the crowd because he wore his hair long and didn't wear a suit shared with the group his desire to meet a woman who could be a partner, but stipulated that he wasn't butch and didn't get the "femme thing." A joke was made in return by a femme woman who stated that of course he didn't get the femme thing. Everyone laughed, even me, until I realized that she wasn't just joking. She proceeded to instruct him about how a woman likes and needs to be treated so that she will feel precious, loved, and feminine. Instead of recognizing his individual reading of masculinity, a reading so significant to him that he physically altered his body to more closely match his vision of himself, she belittled him, unintentionally, for not being a mature butch yet, but merely one in the making. But what if his sense of masculinity has nothing to do with this vogue of butch behavior and conformity? What if it has different roots?

And what if his conception of himself was not necessarily the most ultimate masculine image imaginable, but simply a unique combination? A young woman at the conference asked this question, and I felt relieved and admired her for saying that she herself felt a variety of identities and conformed to none. Everyone makes their own choices, certainly, but many people's choices are narrow and limited in scope. Perhaps some want it that way. One side effect of the concrete gender roles of the 1950s present at the conference, however, was the imposition of strata of gender achievement. Several people in transition expressed their anxiety about being held to standards of hyper-masculinity. The overall feeling of the conference was that conformity was rewarded and individual variation seen as imperfect, as something yet to be perfected.

So I remain skeptical about Pat Califia's claim that butch and femme genders are innate in lesbians. If she had spoken of individual expression, I would adamantly defend the right of every individual to their chosen or acknowledged gender expression. Califia tries to make those who don't subscribe to her view look as if they are ignorant of their own sexual natures. I tend to think it's easy to manipulate people with that kind of argument because many people do not know the boundaries or definitions of their gendered and sexual beings. And yet is that ignorance, or is it the wisdom of not knowing? I would not be so quick to replace the questioning of gender identity the feminist movement opened up with complacency and the false sense of comfort derived from allowing conformity to stand in place for identity. Following a scripted gender, and reacting to one, may intensify a kind of abstract excitement in finally establishing (not revealing) self-identity, but in the end, this is a creation, not something substantial or real. In fact, on some level, it is a decision to act as if one is real and to overlook all evidence to the contrary.

In 1999, a *Lesbian Connection* reader asked other readers for advice about gender identity in the bedroom: "Dear LC, I am a femme who is sometimes mistaken for a soft butch due to my physical strength (I love to work out) and my ability to take an intellectual stance at times."[21] From the start she is appealing to an unstated paradigm that arises any time the ever-absent femme is called into being: the "not" that allows the butch to "be." The femme is expected to shape her identity as the opposite of that of the butch, which is characterized by strength, control, competence, financial independence, and other "male" qualities. A femme, by inference from her statement, is someone who lacks intellectual competence, self-assurance, and physical power. She lacks the power, if you will, to make a firm footprint in the sand. If the confinement of feminine existence to female non-being in relation to men is meant to heighten the masculine subject's sense of omnipotent existence, then in the butch-femme dynamic, it would seem that self-effacement on the part of the femme is even more crucial to establishing a sense of masculinity (being) for the ever-wanting, ever-lacking butch.

However, in the butch/femme paradigm, there may be room to play with subjectivity, given the fact that the woman is the focal point of physical erotic fulfillment in the example just given, hence there seems to be a potential for reaching new territory in sexual communication. The femme in such a case has become the subject in the sexual context. Considering the butch partner's ultimate residence in the female domain, a picture emerges that challenges and in fact overthrows the preexisting paradigm of male domination.

The excitement over this potential for freedom must be countered with the fact that roles can be confining and can detract from conscious presence. Policing assumptions can be made that demand conformity rather than individual expression. For example, one white, working-class woman I know who has friends in academe has been labeled as butch by several of her acquaintances. One wanted her to meet Leslie Feinberg because she was sure they would hit it off, regardless of the fact that she shared none of Feinberg's politics or self-proclaimed feminist tendencies. Another accused her of being "butch on the street, femme in the sheets" because she was not stone butch in her lovemaking. In the first attitude I see an attempt to force a person into a role, in this case seeing her as a noble, heroic figure, like the character Jess in Feinberg's novel. But she herself was not enraptured by this mystique. In the second attitude I see manipulation—a direct effort to force this woman to play a role that the other sees as erotically fulfilling. The role seems to give her power, but in this case it was an attempt to reduce her, to control her, to make her a purely erotic image rather than an individual. Although some people might invite such an opportunity, she did not, and she found it insulting. Her womanhood, her femininity, was being denied, and her characteristics of forthrightness and physical strength were being read as masculine, thus denying her the courtesy of being regarded as a multifaceted woman.

In a slightly different twist on this issue, the letter-writer in *Lesbian Connection* takes to heart her desire to become her lover's fantasy even as she rebels against her partner's attempt to corral her into a defined identity. She polices herself with her own doubts about her right to self-determination. Her letter continues, "My problem is that in the bedroom I somehow seem to often end up on top, much to the displeasure of my soft butch partner. She never attempts to push me off, nor initiate being on top herself, but later says she's not satisfied when I'm in the dominant position." Her partner is asking her to be a little less present in the bedroom, as if by taking up less sexual space she would be less threatening to her sense of control and enjoyment of masculine privilege.

The writer asks, finally, "I'm wondering—isn't there such thing as a soft butch who is strong enough to enjoy her femme being on top once in a while without feeling threatened?"[22] I think her question, once deciphered, is whether she can exist as a post-feminist femme, and the answer is an all-too-obvious, "Why not?" What in the world would keep her, as a woman, from exploring sexual and relationship dynamics with this or any other lover, unless she herself felt the need to conform to the prefeminist ideal of the "femme"? In feminist shorthand, reductive though it might be, she wants to be treated as a precious feminine woman and to maintain a sense of self-determination. The answer to her question seems so obvious in this postfeminist age that it seems puzzling, and it is disheartening that a woman would feel so disempowered that she would question the possibility of existing in the world as an assertive equal partner in a relationship.

In fact, she was probably skating on thin ice within the butch/femme paradigm of the 1990s, because she could very easily be called one of those "reactionary" monsters—a femme who is not satisfied to be put on the pedestal of minimization. Some in butch/femme circles might accuse her of being a confused androgyne, a woman who has lost her womanhood and yet cannot claim masculine authority.

How does a feminist assert herself in the world and still be treated like a woman? This is a question that troubles certain contemporary conservative mainstream heterosexual feminists as well, and a confining ideology may be ruffling feathers for some adherents of the nouveau butch/femme lesbian communities and identity styles. As a feminist, I personally feel that unless we're willing to redefine womanhood in a way that expands the boundaries of femaleness into grounds of subjectivity and self-determination, attempts at liberation while maintaining one's preciousness as a helpless, sexually objectified female creature are bound to fail. And unfortunately, despite the best intentions, some aspects of nouveau butch/femme ideology pave the way, along with its retrograde fashions, back to readings of gender that relegate feminine identity to a limited, circumscribed space in terms of sensual expression and public freedom.

Every choice has consequences. We live in a time as American women when we have extensive freedom in determining our identity. And yet, in the interest of being attractive, of being loved and accepted, many women compromise. I recently attended an evening of films by Islamic women in which one of the speakers on a discussion panel asked why American women see themselves as superior to, as more free than, Muslim women, when in fact they are plagued by self-doubts and anorexia as they squeeze themselves into tight clothes and undergo surgery to attain the narrowly defined body that defines acceptable womanhood within our cultural milieu. Her question illustrates my point that decisions made out of coercion and fear are not free. Our choices concerning gender cannot be made in a vacuum, much as we might wish it were so.

Unlike masculinized identity in women, which might be an innate, perhaps even biologically rooted sense of being, the current butch/femme craze is a fad and a style. The very terms used are archaic and call forth images of James Dean haircuts, rides in an open red convertible on a Saturday night, and a girl trying to keep her virginity while winning a husband. Butch identity is not a cross-cultural experience. The trappings of masculinity are rooted in particular cultural and historical paradigms. It might be a hot image for some people, particularly those who actively seek out scenarios of fantasy, perhaps as S&M practitioners who explore reactions to various empowered and vulnerable positions of partners in fantasized situations. The assumption is that fantasies leave no trace and that butch/femme role-playing, no matter how confining, has a lightness to it that floats above the mundane. If every identity were merely fantasy, holding no weight or consequence, then there would be no need for a feminist struggle. It's all choice. If you don't like being in the woman's role, then choose to be a man. But doesn't such an attitude reinforce these two roles as the only options and at least potentially reinstate the omnipresent historical and cultural assumptions of womanhood as a repressed, objectified, and lesser state? How can any of us, brought up in a society with complex and confused notions of gender, claim objectivity and neutrality in regard to gender?

The appeal that nostalgic butch/femme images hold for young lesbians today is due to a superimposed mystique of badness and forbidden sexuality. The settings in Leslie Feinberg's novel *Stone Butch Blues*, for instance, are dimly lit clubs, sites of illegal and subversive activity. In the same way, underground S&M bars where anything can happen are also the setting for some of Pat Califia's erotic tales. These are outlaw sites where outsiders find a sense of community in resistance and excitement at the prospect of wide-open possibility.

In contrast, the individualism of our times leaves many of us feeling isolated and alone. Many of us feel like misfits and rebels (but sometimes like heroes) who exist in resistance to the system. We embrace our status as outsiders, but perhaps we lack the sense of connectedness we imagine the warrior lawbreakers of the past felt; they knew that their underground meeting places could be raided at any time and their secret world exposed to the scrutiny and criticism of judgmental figures of authority. The current S&M scene similarly continues the battle against controlling forces, and in this respect provides strong support for lesbian identity to become more public and be defiantly present. It seems that a tension exists between the need for community and the need for individuals to find free expression of their gender and sexual identities. However, if respect for individual choice and identity is upheld by members of diverse queer communities, including butch/femme and S&M communities, then prospects for the future look bright.

Conclusion

This treatise focuses on two primary groups of writers and the intersections in the issues they uphold as the foundations of feminist battles in contemporary society. The first group consists of lesbian and transgender feminists. My exploration of writings by authors who focus on transgender, butch/femme, S&M, and other defiantly present lesbian identities begins and ends with an unspoken question: "Is feminism as the politics of personal choice an effective path for personal and social transformation?" The underlying assumption is that the face of feminism today is influenced by newly visible and empowered feminists who seek absolute freedom of self-expression. Rebellious and defiant "warriors" seek emancipation from the shackles of censoring and disheartening societal judgments through self-determining acts in dress, gender presentation, art, and literature. They push the boundaries of sexual expression and gender, keying in on issues that seem, for them, to be at the heart of women's oppression and dehumanization.

The second group I focus on is women of color who write about experiences of racial oppression, and conversely, experiences of personal empowerment through self-determination and defiance of narrow-minded prejudice. In thinking about the messages of a broad array of literature, I came away with the image of a separate space or, to loosely quote the mystical Carlos Casteneda, "a separate reality" that women not only live in but actively create for themselves, and from which they derive empowerment, healing, and the fulfillment of dreams for a better life and a kinder, more caring world. The writings of Maya Angelou, Toni Morrison, and

Audre Lorde come to mind in this regard. In all of the writings I address by these three women, two messages seem to me to run side by side—the immensity and incomprehensible ugliness of pervasive racism and oppression and the glossing over of the effects with placating lies planted in history by institutions and unscrupulous, thoughtless, and selfish individuals. However, in reading their work, even as we feel the breath of these monsters breathing down our necks, a message of hope and transcendence arises.

The hope presented is complicated by the inescapable knowledge of the defeats of history, of ancestors forced to endure enslavement and all its accompanying atrocities, of genocide of cultures and people, and of human lives and dignity laid waste. The avenue through which these authors address feminism is shaped by these realities, and rather than turn away from the painful awareness of historical brutality, they call it forth in order to celebrate the greatness of those who survived and those who survive today in the wake of this horrific knowledge. What rises, for me, from their poetry and prose is a question of what survival is, for even those who have passed away, even those who lost their lives in acts of courageous or compassionate defiance, live on as inspiration to encourage people today to be free of those embracing the ideology of oppression.

Survival, with its layered meanings, has symbolic and not merely physical reality. To die justly, or to die a victim, is not the end of the story if actions are viewed morally, in spirit. Poetically, spirits live on, through stories told and unearthed from the shadows of nameless statistics and distant cultural memories. The nature of this spirit that survives, whether it be religious, poetic, or literal, fascinates me, for it is from this view that I approach the ghost survivors at the end of *Paradise* and the cultural memories that fuel Maya's indefatigable self-esteem and self-generated strength in *I Know Why a Caged Bird Sings*. Likewise, Native American author Mable McKay's story of her connection to "spirit" and the living traditions of the past for the Pomo people calls forth a sense of survival that cannot be defeated by the story told by the oppressors. These are competing realities: what the forces in power fear as chaos and the downfall of civilization others may view as the infinite myriad of perspectives that intertwine in existence. The message I see is that there is something transcendent that cannot be obliterated.

When I began writing, I wasn't sure there was a connection between these two groups of feminist writers—those who dismantle gender outsider/outlaw status and those who dismantle racial marginalization. I was aware only that contemporary feminism has been broadened by the perspectives of these two groups. Then I began to focus more concretely on survival and the idea of separate space and defiant identity. For some of the fictional characters and real authors I address, defiance is a conscious and passionate, perhaps even violent (as in the case of S&M theorists), act of overthrowing the oppressive force of censoring patriarchy by acting out the individual will of self-expression so long denied women. For others, merely to exist is an act of defiance in the face of the hatred of those who deny the rights of subjective consciousness and even physical existence for any but themselves. This desperate state of affairs applies to transgender fictional characters and to characters who face racist violence.

Survival and space, in the end, are relative for the individual who must survive in a broader context of the threat of annihilation of self and space in every figurative and literal sense. Survival is in no way a given for the poor or for those who are subject to racial or gender oppression. And yet the hope of survival remains, and must remain, for hope itself seems to be the source of survival, the sustaining and strengthening root and trunk that allow the individual to declare that she (and he) will survive even against seemingly impossible odds. The policing state, no matter how restrictive and brutal, cannot suppress every act of defiance. The acts arise again and again, born from ever more individuals. And so acts of defiance born of courage and necessity push forth the rights of the individual to dignity, freedom from violence, and the right to existence and self-expression.

Literature, like all expressive artistic and political acts, can be both transgressive and transformative. I have attempted to present an array of approaches that are being acted out on the broad field of contemporary feminism. These acts of defiant self-affirmation are enacted in some cases by authors and literary characters and by performers, cartoonists, women's festival attendees, and so on. I have attempted to treat literature as a template for contemporary feminist experience and have tried to unearth the complex and multidimensional approaches to feminism espoused by various writers and contemporary feminists.

In the end, I suppose I am offering a definition of contemporary feminism as a broad coalition of differing needs and interests, connected by a common thread of the desire for self-respect and self-determination for all human beings, including women, and a desire for a compassionate approach to community and government. In the images I presented of the Michigan Womyn's Music Festival and the philosophical debates taking place among the organizers and attendees, I was revealing in a microcosm the difficulties I see in ever defining feminism in a fixed, exclusive manner. The shape of feminism changes with the times, and it is shaped by the particular perspectives, needs, and experiences of every individual.

I believe that personal transformation, self-education, and empowerment are powerful feminist tools. My view of the contemporary feminist movement's embrace of individualism is hopeful, yet I am fearful of a splintering of aims and progress unless the goals of women as a unified community are made clear. The tool of political cohesiveness should not be wielded to exclude the concerns of those whose voices contradict, at times, the needs of a vocal majority. There is no possibility of defining feminism except in a reductive and inadequate manner. The fascinating and living entanglement of the voices of our times, as long as we are all willing to listen to each other, creates a space where difference is not devastating and divisive but is rather an enhancing force with the potential to expand awareness of new perspectives, even those which we may struggle. For instance, S&M might not be everyone's cup of tea, but those writers, theorists, artists, and other individuals who embrace that lifestyle might well have something to say to almost any feminist willing to listen.

In the many and varied approaches to feminism I have incorporated in this work, a common ground may be found in the awareness of oppression, even with the understanding that specific cultural groups face particular kinds and degrees of oppression. I believe there is a commonality linking the authors I have presented as feminists, even if it is a loose net and many types of perception exist. I would like to believe that our society as a whole is gradually transforming for the better, or at least that the potential for improvement, for intelligent and compassionate communication and existence, exists, despite the seemingly insurmountable obstacles.

Clearly, there is no one "feminism," and yet the links between varying viewpoints exist. As a bastion against one form of oppression, feminism can be understood as a focal point in the battle against all oppressions. It is not the only focal point, and yet it remains pivotal, just as the survival of every individual has meaning for the larger community as a whole. Personal acts of courage, defiance, and self-empowerment strengthen us all.

Notes

Introduction

1. Audre Lorde, "Poetry Is Not a Luxury," in *Sister Outsider: Essays and Speeches* (Trumansburg, NY: Crossing Press, 1984), 36.

1. Twentieth-Century Multicultural Women Writers of North America

1. Christina Hoff Sommers, *Who Stole Feminism? How Women Have Betrayed Women* (New York: Touchstone), 22.
2. Judith Butler, *Bodies That Matter: On the Discursive Limits of Sex* (New York: Routledge, 1993), 181.
3. Butler, *Bodies That Matter,* 183–184.
4. Sarah Orne Jewett, "The Landscape Chamber," in *Deephaven and Other Stories* (New Haven, CT: College and University Press, 1966), 188.
5. Lillian Faderman, *Chloe Plus Olivia* (New York: Viking, 1994), 96–98.
6. Sarah Orne Jewett, "The White Heron," in *Deephaven and Other Stories* (New Haven, CT: College and University Press, 1966), 204.
7. Willa Cather, *A Lost Lady* (New York: Vintage Books, 1994), 17.
8. Faderman, *Chloe Plus Olivia,* 236.
9. Cather, *A Lost Lady,* 25.
10. Faderman, *Chloe Plus Olivia,* 239.
11. Butler, *Bodies That Matter,* 181–195.
12. Howard Zinn, *A People's History of the United States* (New York: HarperPerennial, 1995), 6–7.

13. Esmerelda Santiago, *When I Was Puerto Rican* (New York: Vintage Books, 1993), 250.
14. Charlotte Templin, "The Male-Dominated Curriculum in English: How Did We Get Here and Where Are We Going?" in *Feminism and the Politics of Literary Reputation: The Example of Erica Jong* (Lawrence, KS: University Press of Kansas, 1995), 30–47.

2. Butch/Femme Relationships in Works of Fiction

1. Sandra Bem, *The Lenses of Gender* (New Haven: Yale University Press, 1993), 41.
2. American Psychiatric Association, *DSM*-III (Washington, D.C.: American Psychiatric Association, 1980); Bem, *The Lenses of Gender*, 93-94; and http://psychology.ucdavis.edu/rainbow/html/facts-mental-health.html.
3. http://psychology.ucdavis.edu/rainbow/html/facts-mental-health.html.
4. Bem, *The Lenses of Gender*, 95.
5. http://psychology.ucdavis.edu/rainbow/html/resolutions97.html.
6. Allison Soutter, "A Longitudinal Study of Three Cases of Gender Identity Disorder of Childhood Successfully Resolved in the School Setting," *School Psychology International* 17, no. 1 (February 1996), 49-50.
7. bell hooks, "Power to the Pussy," in *Outlaw Culture: Resisting Representation* (New York: Routledge, 1994), 19.
8. Judith Butler, *Gender Trouble* (New York: Routledge, 1990), 334.
9. Ibid., 337.
10. Ibid.
11. Minnie Bruce Pratt, *S/HE* (Ithaca, New York: Firebrand Press, 1995), 19.
12. Ibid., 137.
13. Claudia Brenner, *Eight Bullets* (Ithaca, New York: Firebrand Press, 1994).
14. Pratt, *S/HE*, 123.
15. Ibid., 135–136.
16. Ibid., 131.
17. http://www.transgenderwarrior.org.

18. Riki Anne Wilchins, *Read My Lips: Sexual Subversion and the End of Gender* (Ithaca, NY: Firebrand Books, 1997), 24.
19. Judith Halberstam, "Between Butches," in *Butch/Femme: Inside Lesbian Gender*, ed. Sally Munt (London: Cassell Press, 1998), 88.
20. Leslie Feinberg, *Stone Butch Blues* (Ithaca, NY: Firebrand Books, 1993), 175.
22. Marjorie Garber, *Vested Interests* (New York: HarperCollins, 1992), 101-102.
21. Leslie Feinberg, *Stone Butch Blues* (Ithaca, NY: Firebrand Books, 1993), 195.
23. Ibid., 193.
24. Audre Lorde, "Uses of the Erotic," in *Sister Outsider: Essays and Speeches* (Trumansburg, NY: Crossing Press, 1984), 55.
25. Frankie Hucklenbroich, *A Crystal Diary* (Ithaca, New York: Firebrand Press, 1997), 157.
25. Ibid., 185.

3. Progressive Confrontation

1. Audre Lorde, "The Master's Tools Will Never Dismantle the Master's House," in *Sister Outsider: Essays and Speeches* (Trumansburg, NY: Crossing Press, 1984), 110.
2. Ibid., 111.
3. Lisa Vogel, public letter, *Lesbian Connection* (November/December 1999), 5.
4. Ibid., 6.
5. "Bosom foes together again" Sunday Styles Section, *New York Times*, 3 May 1988.
6. In *Ms. Magazine*, (May-June 1998) 8, no. 6: 29.
7. Amy Aronson, "Cybill Shepherd Interview," in *Ms. Magazine* (March-April 1998) 8, no. 5: 68.
8. Susan Bordo, *Twilight Zones: The Hidden Lives of Cultural Images from Plato to O.J.* (Berkeley: University of California Press, 1997), 186.
9. Diane DiMassa, *Hothead Paisan: Homocidal Lesbian Terrorist* (San Francisco: Cleis Press, 1993), 50–51.
10. Ibid., 42–43.
11. Bordo, *Twilight Zones*, 187.

12. Anna M. Cox, Freya Johnson, Annalee Newitz, and Jillian Sandell, "Masculinity Without Men: Women Reconciling Feminism and Male Identification," in *Third Wave Agenda: Being Feminist, Doing Feminism*, ed. Leslie Heywood and Jennifer Drake (Minneapolis: University of Minnesota, 1997), 184.
13. Ibid., 187–187, 191.
14. Alison Bechdel, *Dykes to Watch Out For: The Sequel* (Ithaca, NY: Firebrand Press, 1992), 109, 132–133.
15. Julia Knight, "The Meaning of Treut?" in *Immortal, Invisible: Lesbians and the Moving Image*, ed. Tamsin Wilton (New York: Routledge, 1995), 46.
16. Ibid.
17. bell hooks, "Moving Into and Beyond Feminism," in *Outlaw Culture: Resisting Representation* (New York: Routledge, 1994), 213.
18. Audre Lorde, "Sadomasochism: Not About Condemnation," in *A Burst of Light* (Ithaca, NY: Firebrand Press, 1988).

4. Resistance and Liberation

1. Audre Lorde, "Poetry Is Not a Luxury," in *Sister Outsider: Essays and Speeches* (Trumansburg, NY: Crossing Press, 1984), 39.
2. Jeffrey Elliot, *Conversations with Maya Angelou* (Jackson, MS: University of Mississippi Press, 1989), 220.
3. Carolyn Forché, *The Country Between Us* (Philadelphia: Harper and Row, 1981), 20.
4. Ibid.
5. Ibid., 17.
6. Ibid., 16.
7. Betty Bao Lord, *Legacies: A Chinese Mosaic* (New York: Knopf, 1990), 3.
8. Howard Zinn, *A People's History of the United States* (New York: HarperPerennial, 1995), 7.
9. Ibid., 167, 514.
10. Carlson Vicenti, "Hitching," in *Neon Pow-Wow: New Native American Voices of the Southwest* (Flagstaff, AZ: Northland Pub., 1993), 12.
11. Ibid.
12. Joseph Marshall, III, "Cozy by the Fire," in *The Dance House: Stories from Rosebud* (Santa Fe, NM: Red Crane Books, 1998), 28.
13. Ibid., 35.

14. Ibid., 37–48.
15. Black Elk, *Black Elk Speaks* (Lincoln: University of Nebraska Press, 1932), 20–47.
16. Ibid., 242.
17. Dalai Lama, *My Land and My People* (New York: Warner Books, 1997), 47.
18. Ibid., 41–42.
19. Situ Rinpoche, Informal discussion at Sherab Ling Monastery, Himachel Pradesh, India, 1990.
20. Dalai Lama, *My Land and My People*, 190, 196.
21. Ibid., 212.
22. Wallace Black Elk, *Black Elk: The Sacred Ways of the Lakota* (San Francisco: HarperCollins Publishers, 1990),122.
23. Joseph Marshall, III, "Oliver's Silver Dollar," in *The Dance House: Stories from Rosebud* (Santa Fe, NM: Red Crane Books, 1998), 22.
24. Ibid., 1.
25. Ibid., 12.
26. Black Elk, *Black Elk*, 123.
27. Ibid., 124.
28. Ibid., 124–125.
29. Ibid., 125.
30. Ibid., 128.
31. Greg Sarris, *Mable McKay: Weaving the Dream* (Berkeley: University of California Press, 1994), 31.
32. Ibid., 20.
33. Ibid., 33.
34. Ibid., 23–26.
35. Ibid., 42.
36. Ibid., 73.
37. Ibid., 74–76.
38. Ibid., 109.
39. Ibid., 111.
40. Ibid., 112.
41. Ibid., 113.
42. Maya Angelou, *I Know Why the Caged Bird Sings* (New York: Bantam Books, 1969), 121.

43. Ibid.
44. Ibid., 123.
45. Ibid., 127.
46. Ibid.
47. Ibid., 129, 131.
48. Cornel West, " Black Culture and Postmodernism," *Remaking History*, eds. Barbara Kruger and Phil Mariani (San Francisco: Bay Press, 1989), 92.
49. Ibid.
50. Ibid., 394.
51. Angelou, *I Know Why*, 8.
52. Ibid., 30.
53. Barbara Smith, "A Rose," in *The Truth That Never Hurts: Writings on Race, Gender, and Freedom* (New Brunswick, NJ: Rutgers University Press, 1998), 192–193.
54. Maya Angelou, *Wouldn't Take Nothing for My Journey Now* (New York: Random House, 1993), 64.

5. Expanding the Parameters of Feminism

1. Audre Lorde, "Poetry Is Not a Luxury," in *Sister Outsider: Essays and Speeches* (Trumansburg, NY: Crossing Press, 1984), 39.
2. Toni Morrison, *Paradise* (New York: Alfred Knopf, 1998), 26.
3. Ibid., 25.
4. Audre Lorde, "Uses of the Erotic," in *Sister Outsider: Essays and Speeches* (Trumansburg, NY: Crossing Press, 1984), 53.
5. Ibid., 55.
6. Morrison, *Paradise*, 18.
7. Ibid., 94.
8. Ibid., 314.

6. The Transformative Power of Personal Voice

1. Adrienne Rich, "Invisibility in Academe," in *Blood, Bread, and Poetry: Selected Prose 1979-1985* (New York: W.W. Norton & Company, 1986), 199.

2. Audre Lorde, "Poetry Is Not a Luxury," in *Sister Outsider: Essays and Speeches* (Trumansburg, NY: Crossing Press, 1984), 37.
3. Leslea Newman, *Writing from the Heart: Inspiration and Exercises for Women Who Want to Write* (Freedom, CA: The Crossing Press, 1993), 1.
4. Toni Morrison, *Paradise* (New York: Alfred Knopf, 1998), 81–138.
5. Susan Bordo, *Twilight Zones: The Hidden Lives of Cultural Images from Plato to O.J.* (Berkeley: University of California Press, 1997), 84.
6. bell hooks, "Building a Teaching Community," in *Teaching to Transgress* (New York: Routledge, 1994), 142.
7. Bordo, *Twilight Zones*, 82.
8. Howard Zinn, *The Zinn Reader* (New York: Seven Stories Press, 1997), 569.
9. bell hooks, Introduction, in *Teaching to Transgress* (New York: Routledge, 1994), 8.

7. Reflections on Alternative Identities in Contemporary Feminism

1. Pat Califia, *Melting Point* (Los Angeles: Alyson Publications, 1993), 231.
2. Ibid.
3. Consuelo Concepcion, "On Pornography, Representation, and Sexual Agency," *Hypatia* 14, no. 1 (Winter 1999), 98.
4. Ibid., 99.
5. Alisa Carse, "Pornography's Many Meanings: A Reply to C. M. Concepcion," *Hypatia* 14, no. 1 (Winter 1999), 101.
6. Ibid., 102.
7. Ibid., 103.
8. Ibid., 105.
9. Rose Tremain, *Sacred Country* (New York: Washington Square Press, 1992), 145.
10. Ibid., 29.
11. Ibid., 185.
12. Ibid., 5.
13. Ibid., 102.

14. Ibid., 130.
15. Ibid.
16. Ibid., 112–113.
17. Ibid., 133.
18. Ibid., 177.
19. Ibid., 232.
20. Pat Califia, Advice Column, *GirlTalk* 5, no. 6 (June 1999), 46.
21. Letter to the Editor, *Lesbian Connection* 22, no. 2 (September-October 1999).
22. Ibid., 11.

Bibliography

Alley, Kirstie. Quoted in "On the Record" section, excerpted from *US Magazine* (January 1998) in *Ms. Magazine* (May-June 1998) VIII, no. 6.

Angelou, Maya. *I Know Why the Caged Bird Sings.* New York: Bantam Books, 1969.

———. *Wouldn't Take Nothing for My Journey Now.* New York: Random House, 1993.

Anonymous. Letter to Editor, *Lesbian Connection* (September-October 1999) 22, no. 2.

Aronson, Amy. "Cybill Shepherd Interview." In *Ms. Magazine* (March–April 1998) 8, no. 5: 68.

Atwood, Margaret. *Cat's Eye.* New York: Anchor Books, 1998.

Bechdel, Alison. *Dykes to Watch Out For: The Sequel.* Ithaca, NY: Firebrand Press, 1992.

Bem, Sandra. *The Lenses of Gender.* New Haven: Yale University Press, 1993.

Black Elk. *Black Elk Speaks.* Lincoln: University of Nebraska Press, 1932.

Black Elk, Wallace. *Black Elk: The Sacred Ways of the Lakota.* San Francisco: HarperCollins Publishers, 1990.

Bordo, Susan. *Twilight Zones: The Hidden Lives of Cultural Images from Plato to O.J.* Berkeley: University of California Press, 1997.

Brenner, Claudia. *Eight Bullets.* Ithaca, New York: Firebrand Press, 1994.

Butler, Judith. *Bodies That Matter: On the Discursive Limits of Sex.* New York: Routledge, 1993.

———. *Gender Trouble*. New York: Routledge, 1990.

Califia, Pat. *Melting Point*. Los Angeles: Alyson Publications, 1993.

Carse, Alisa. "Pornography's Many Meanings: A Reply to C. M. Concepcion." *Hypatia* 14, no. 1 (Winter 1999).

Cather, Willa. *A Lost Lady*. New York: Vintage Books, 1994.

Concepcion, Consuelo. "On Pornography, Representation, and Sexual Agency," *Hypatia* 14, no. 1 (Winter 1999).

Conde, Maryse. *I Tituba, Black Witch of Salem*. Translated by Richard Philcox. Charlottesville: University Press of Virginia, 1992.

Cox, Anna M.; Johnson, Freya; Newitz, Annalee; Sandell, Jillian. "Masculinity Without Men: Women Reconciling Feminism and Male Identification," in *Third Wave Agenda: Being Feminist, Doing Feminism*, ed. Leslie Heywood and Jennifer Drake. Minneapolis: University of Minnesota, 1997.

Dalai Lama. *My Land and My People*. New York: Warner Books, 1997.

DiMassa, Diane. *Hothead Paisan: Homocidal Lesbian Terrorist*. San Francisco: Cleis Press, 1993.

Elliot, Jeffrey. *Conversations with Maya Angelou*. Jackson, MS: University of Mississippi Press, 1989.

Faderman, Lillian. *Chloe Plus Olivia*. New York: Viking, 1994.

Feinberg, Leslie. *Stone Butch Blues: A Novel*. Ithaca, NY: Firebrand Books, 1993.

Forché, Carolyn. *The Country between Us*. Philadelphia: Harper and Row, 1981.

Garber, Marjorie. *Vested Interests*. New York: HarperCollins, 1992.

Halberstam, Judith. "Between Butches." In *Butch/Femme: Inside Lesbian Gender*, ed. Sally Munt. London: Cassell Press, 1998.

hooks, bell. "Building a Teaching Community." In *Teaching to Transgress*. New York: Routledge, 1994.

———. Introduction. In *Teaching to Transgress*. New York: Routledge, 1994.

———. "Moving Into and Beyond Feminism." In *Outlaw Culture: Resisting Representation*. New York: Routledge, 1994.

———. "Power to the Pussy." In *Outlaw Culture: Resisting Representation*. New York: Routledge, 1994.

Hucklenbroich, Frankie. *A Crystal Diary*. Ithaca, New York: Firebrand Press, 1997.

Jewett, Sarah Orne. *Delphanen and Other Stories*. New Haven, CT: College and University Press, 1966.

Knight, Julia. "The Meaning of Treut?" In *Immortal, Invisible: Lesbians and the Moving Image*, ed. Tamsin Wilton. New York: Routledge, 1995.

Lord, Betty Bao. *Legacies: A Chinese Mosaic*. New York: Knopf, 1990.

Lorde, Audre. "The Master's Tools Will Never Dismantle the Master's House." In *Sister Outsider: Essays and Speeches*. Trumansburg, NY: Crossing Press, 1984.

———. "Poetry Is Not a Luxury." In *Sister Outsider: Essays and Speeches*. Trumansburg, NY: Crossing Press, 1984.

———. "Sadomasochism: Not About Condemnation." In *A Burst of Light*. Ithaca, NY: Firebrand Press, 1988.

———. "Uses of the Erotic." In *Sister Outsider: Essays and Speeches*. Trumansburg, NY: Crossing Press, 1984.

MacDonald, Anne-Marie. *Fall on Your Knees*. New York: Simon & Schuster, 1996.

Marshall, III, Joseph. "Cozy by the Fire." In *The Dance House: Stories from Rosebud*. Santa Fe, NM: Red Crane Books, 1998.

———. "Oliver's Silver Dollar." In *The Dance House: Stories from Rosebud*. Santa Fe, NM: Red Crane Books, 1998.

Monroe, Alice. *The Beggar Maid: Stories of Flo and Rose*. New York: Penguin, 1980.

Morrison, Toni. *Beloved: A Novel*. New York: A.A. Knopf, 1993.

———. *The Bluest Eye*. New York: Alfred Knopf, 1993.

———. *Paradise*. New York: Knopf, 1998.

Newman, Leslea. *Writing from the Heart: Inspiration and Exercises for Women Who Want to Write*. Freedom, CA: The Crossing Press, 1993.

Pratt, Minnie Bruce. *S/HE*. Ithaca, New York: Firebrand Press, 1995.

Rich, Adrienne. "Invisibility in Academe," in *Blood, Bread, and Poetry: Selected Prose 1979-1985*. New York: W.W. Norton & Company, 1986.

Santiago, Esmerelda. *When I Was Puerto Rican*. New York: Vintage Books, 1993.

Sarris, Greg. *Mable McKay: Weaving the Dream.* Berkeley: University of California Press, 1994.

Situ Rinpoche, Informal discussion at Sherab Ling Monastery, Himachel Pradesh, India, 1990.

Smith, Barbara. "A Rose." In *The Truth That Never Hurts: Writings on Race, Gender, and Freedom.* New Brunswick, NJ: Rutgers University Press, 1998.

Sommers, Christina Hoff. *Who Stole Feminism? How Women Have Betrayed Women.* New York: Simon & Schuster, 1994.

Soutter, Allison. "A Longitudinal Study of Three Cases of Gender Identity Disorder of Childhood Successfully Resolved in the School Setting." *School Psychology International* 17, no. 1 (February 1996).

Steinem, Gloria. Quoted in "Bosom Foes Together Again." Sunday Styles Section, *New York Times*, 3 May 1988.

Templin, Charlotte. "The Male-Dominated Curriculum in English: How Did We Get Here and Where Are We Going?" in *Feminism and the Politics of Literary Reputation: The Example of Erica Jong.* Lawrence, KS: University Press of Kansas, 1995.

Tremain, Rose. *Sacred Country.* New York: Washington Square Press, 1992.

Vicenti, Carlson. "Hitching." In *Neon Pow-Wow: New Native American Voices of the Southwest.* Flagstaff, AZ: Northland Pub., 1993.

Vogel, Lisa. Public letter in *Lesbian Connection*, November/December, 1999.

West, Cornel. "Black Culture and Postmodernism." In *Remaking History*, eds. Barbara Kruger and Phil Mariani. San Francisco: Bay Press, 1989.

Wilchins, Riki Anne. *Read My Lips: Sexual Subversion and the End of Gender.* Ithaca, NY: Firebrand Books, 1997.

Yamanaha, Lois-Ann. *Wild Meat and the Bully Burgers.* New York: Farrar Straus Giroux, 1996.

Zinn, Howard. *A People's History of the United States.* New York: Harper Collins, 1995.

———. *The Zinn Reader.* New York: Seven Stories Press, 1997.

ERUPTIONS
New Thinking across the Disciplines

Erica McWilliam
General Editor

This is a series of red-hot women's writing after the "isms." It focuses on new cultural assemblages that are emerging from the de-formation, breakout, ebullience, and discomfort of postmodern feminism. The series brings together a post-foundational generation of women's writing that, while still respectful of the idea of situated knowledge, does not rely on neat disciplinary distinctions and stable political coalitions. This writing transcends some of the more awkward textual performances of a first generation of "feminism-meets-postmodernism" scholarship. It has come to terms with its own body of knowledge as shifty, inflammatory, and ungovernable.

The aim of the series is to make this cutting edge thinking more readily available to undergraduate and postgraduate students, researchers and new academics, and professional bodies and practitioners. Thus, we seek contributions from writers whose unruly scholastic projects are expressed in texts that are accessible and seductive to a wider academic readership.

Proposals and/or manuscripts are invited from the domains of: "post" humanities, human movement studies, sexualities, media studies, literary criticism, information technologies, history of ideas, performing arts, gay and lesbian studies, cultural studies, post-colonial studies, pedagogics, social psychology, and the philosophy of science. We are particularly interested in publishing research and scholarship with international appeal from Australia, New Zealand, and the United Kingdom.

For further information about the series and for the submission of manuscripts, please contact:

Erica McWilliam
Faculty of Education
Queensland University of Technology
Victoria Park Rd., Kelvin Grove Q 4059
Australia

To order other books in this series, please contact our Customer Service Department at:

(800) 770-LANG (within the U.S.)
(212) 647-7706 (outside the U.S.)
(212) 647-7707 FAX

Or browse online by series at:

www.peterlangusa.com